# The Real Family Camping Cookbook

# RAVE REVIEWS
## FOR
# THE REAL FAMILY CAMPING COOKBOOK

"Maggie da Silva has a cool blog and a cookbook devoted to the joys of family camping meals. Some smart ideas in here for summer hijinks on the road."

– *The New York Times*

---

"An excellent planning guide, worthy of regular consultation and filled with family-friendly dishes that are quick and easy to reproduce at the campfire."

– *Midwest Book Review*

---

"For delicious cooking tips (and humorous wording) check out the well-reviewed *The Real Family Camping Cookbook* by Maggie da Silva. It is filled with over 150 family-tested camping recipes and musings that are sure to please the palate and funny bone of both little and big campers."

– *The Times-Picayune*

---

"A must-have for families considering a camping trip this summer. From first-time campers (especially) to seasoned veterans, there are recipes in this book that will please everyone in the family. My favorite part of the book is reading recipes that I never (in a million years) would have dreamt up but that make perfect sense when camping!"

– *The Blended Family Blog*

---

"This book will spice up your campsite cooking like no other."

– *Camping in Spain Blog*

# The Real Family Camping Cookbook

MAGGIE DA SILVA

Copyright © 2020 by Maggie da Silva
All rights reserved.
ISBN: 979-8-6892-8206-0

# TABLE OF CONTENTS

| | |
|---|---|
| *Introduction* | 1 |
| *Recipes and Menus* | 3 |
| BREAKFAST | 5 |
| Eggs | 7 |
| French Toast and Pancakes | 30 |
| Fruit and Cereal | 34 |
| SOUP, SIDES, STARTERS and SNACKS | 41 |
| Soup and Sides | 43 |
| Starters | 70 |
| Snacks | 78 |
| MAIN DISHES | 85 |
| Sandwiches | 87 |
| Pie Iron Combos | 95 |
| Foil Packets | 97 |
| Quesadillas, Burritos and Tacos | 99 |
| Pasta | 102 |
| Meat Dishes | 110 |
| Stews and One-Pot Meals | 130 |
| Seafood | 150 |
| Bonus Chicken Recipes | 156 |
| BREADS AND DESSERTS | 163 |
| Breads and Coffee Cakes | 165 |
| Desserts | 169 |
| MEAL PLANS | 203 |
| Acknowledgments | 206 |

This book is dedicated to Pete, Holly, David and Peter,
for all the unforgettable camping adventures.

# The Real Family Camping Cookbook

# INTRODUCTION

This book grew out of our fun food experiments on family camping trips over the years – I liked to try out new dishes on the kids and then write down the recipes back at home to remember for the next time. Eventually, I put together meal plans before our camping trips, which resulted in us eating a wider variety of foods at the campsite – even fruits and vegetables! I was also able to remember to pack for our favorites, like Monkey Bread and Paper Bag Eggs. And over time we stopped overshopping, which saved money and precious cooler space.

Most of these recipes are easy to make and some of them even call for pre-made foods, like refrigerated biscuit dough. For us, camping is all about pitching a tent, hiking, swimming and sitting around the campfire. So if you're like us, you want to spend your time doing that, not beating egg whites and kneading bread. Our camping food is yummy, but it's also easy and fast – and fast and easy to clean up, too.

There are all kinds of campers and camping is for everyone, from experienced hikers with minimalist gear to RVers who bring the comforts of home with them wherever they go. We like to car camp, stuffing everything into the car and chugging to the nearest state park. Once there, we unpack, set up our tent and enjoy the great outdoors – with access to bathrooms, showers and occasionally, a swimming pool!

Cooking at the campsite is part *Little House on the Prairie* and part science experiment. Mostly it's about having fun – which means dishing up the old favorites and trying out new things. I hope this book adds to the fun.

*Maggie*

MAGGIE DA SILVA

## RECIPES AND MENUS

MAGGIE DA SILVA

# BREAKFAST

*Paper Bag Eggs!*

MAGGIE DA SILVA

# EGGS

**Paper Bag Eggs**

No skillet? No pot? Never fear. Another classic recipe for the kids.

*Serves: 1*

*Ingredients:*
2 strips fatty bacon
1 egg
salt & pepper, hot sauce and catsup
1 paper lunch bag
1 green, pointy stick

*Preparation:*
1. Cut both bacon strips in half, giving you 4 pieces. Line the bottom of the paper lunch bag with the bacon to make a nice, fatty bacon nest for the egg.
2. Crack an egg into the nest.
3. Fold the top of the paper bag down carefully 2 times and poke a hole through the thick part with the stick.
4. Carefully hold the bag over the fire so the bacon cooks slowly and the fat melts. This makes an oily paper and bacon "skillet" for the egg. Take care and keep cooking it until the egg is done.
5. Eat it out of the bag ... but put it on a plate! If you put it on your knee it will ruin your pants. I learned this the hard way.
6. Serve with salt & pepper, catsup & hot sauce.

*Variation:*
- Add a handful of frozen hash browns or finely chopped cooked potatoes over the bacon but under the egg.

"Good food ends with good talk." – Geoffrey Neighbor, *Northern Exposure*

## Bacon and Eggs

We generally start every morning with bacon; It makes the campsite smell good and lines our stomachs with a nice basecoat of fat.

*Serves: 4*

*Ingredients:*
8 eggs
8 strips bacon
salt & pepper, hot sauce and catsup

*Preparation:*
1. Chop the bacon and fry it in a skillet.
2. Wipe out some of the fat with a paper towel and return the bacon to the skillet.
3. Beat the eggs and add them to the bacon. Cook over medium heat.
4. After about 2 minutes, flip the whole thing over and cook it another minute or so on the other side.
5. Serve with salt & pepper, catsup and hot sauce.

*Variations:*
- Add some chopped onions, green or red peppers or mushrooms.
- Add a couple of slices of bread, torn into little pieces.
- Add some shredded cheese or little pieces of cream cheese.
- Add a couple of spoonfuls of salsa when the eggs are still soft, and mix it in.
- Instead of bacon, use sliced, leftover hot dogs or kielbasa. You can use hamburger, too, but I can't get used to eating hamburger for breakfast.
- Serve with a warm tortilla.
- Try crushed crackers on top of your eggs, like Saltines, Cheez-Its or Ritz crackers.

"There is no love sincerer than the love of food." – George Bernard Shaw, *Man and Superman*

## Black-Eyed Susan (AKA Man in a Hat AKA Toad in a Hole AKA Egg on a Raft)

We make these two-at-a-time in our big skillet.

*Serves: 2*

*Ingredients:*
2 eggs
2 slices whole grain bread
butter or bacon fat
salt & pepper, hot sauce and catsup

*Preparation:*
1. Cut a hole in the center of the bread with a small jar or a circle cookie cutter, or just rip it as neatly as you can with your fingers. If you want to get fancy, bring fun-shaped cookie cutters and cut a star, etc.
2. Melt 1T. of butter in a skillet. Drop in the bread and crack an egg into the hole in the bread.
3. Cook the egg and bread until it's done on one side, then flip the whole thing over to cook on other side. Fry the bread "holes" at the same time.
4. Serve with salt & pepper, hot sauce and catsup.
5. Repeat as necessary! Bon appétit!

*Variations:*
- After you flip the egg/bread, sprinkle on some shredded cheese and let it melt.
- Add a slice of ham on top of the egg and under the cheese.
- Put a round piece of cooked sausage into the hole before you break the egg into it – it will cook into the egg. Or you can put in some crumbled, cooked bacon.

"I don't like gourmet cooking or 'this' cooking or 'that' cooking. I like good cooking." – James Beard

## Boiled Scrambled Eggs AKA Eggs in a Baggie

Mmm … eggs in a plastic bag. It's a classic!

*Serves: 2*

*Ingredients:*
4 eggs
2 strips bacon
butter
salt & pepper, hot sauce and catsup
2 plastic Ziploc baggies – the large sandwich bag size

*Preparation:*
1. Bring a large pot of water to a boil.
2. Fry the bacon in a skillet.
3. Let each kid tear apart or crumble their bacon into a Ziploc bag.
4. Add a shake each of salt & pepper.
5. Break 2 eggs into each bag and zipper it tightly.
6. Let the kids squish the eggs around until they're scrambled.
7. Open a corner of the bag and squeeze out all of the air so the bags don't explode when you cook them. I learned this the hard way.
8. Put the zipped bags of eggs into a pot of boiling water and cook them until they're done, about 5 minutes.
9. Empty the omelets out of their bags onto plates.
10. Serve with salt & pepper, hot sauce and catsup.

*Variations:*
- Instead of bacon, use cubes of ham or cooked breakfast sausages (or leftover dinner sausages).
- Add cheese.
- Add chopped onions, mushrooms and green or red peppers.
- Serve on a tortilla.
- Garnish with sour cream and salsa or chopped tomato.

"There ain't no such thing as a wrong food." – Sean Stewart, *Perfect Circle*

## Cowboy Eggs

It's not camping unless you have Cowboy Eggs at least one morning.

*Serves: 4*

*Ingredients:*
8 strips bacon
8 eggs, lightly beaten
2 raw potatoes, diced, or 1.5 c. of frozen hash browns
½ small, yellow onion, chopped
¼ each green and a red pepper, chopped
8 white mushrooms, sliced
4 oz. shredded cheese, like Jack or Cheddar
paprika
salt & pepper, hot sauce and catsup

*Preparation:*
1. Chop the bacon, cook it and set it aside.
2. Cook the onions and potatoes in the bacon fat for about 10 minutes.
3. Add the mushrooms and the other veggies and cook for about 5 minutes.
4. Add the eggs and cheese and add back the bacon. Cook until the eggs are done.
5. Sprinkle with paprika. (Potatoes like paprika.)
6. Serve with salt & pepper, catsup and hot sauce.

*Variations:*
- Omit the eggs and you have potato and veggie hash.
- Use sausage instead of bacon … or use both!
- Serve with BBQ sauce or A1 sauce.
- Omit the veggies, cheese and paprika and serve with maple syrup.

"We plan, we toil, we suffer – in the hope of what? A camel-load of idol's eyes? The title deeds of Radio City? The empire of Asia? A trip to the moon? No, no, no, no. Simply to wake just in time to smell coffee and bacon and eggs." – J.B. Priestly

## Eggs Mc(Insert Your Family Name Here)

Camping McMuffins. We cook these like Eggs in a Baggie, but you can cook these in a skillet, too.

*Serves: 2*

*Ingredients:*
2 eggs
2 strips bacon, or another delicious breakfast meat
butter
2 English muffins
2 slices American cheese
salt & pepper, hot sauce and catsup

*Preparation:*
1. Fry the bacon in a skillet.
2. Prepare the eggs per the Eggs in a Baggie method, adding the cooked bacon to the baggie of eggs before it goes into the boiling water.
3. Toast 2 English muffins on the grill, and butter them.
4. Slide the cooked eggs and bacon onto the bottom halves of the English muffins.
5. Add a slice of American cheese.
6. Put the top halves of the English Muffins on top.
7. Serve with salt & pepper, catsup and hot sauce.
8. Take a short nap to let the fat seep into your nooks and crannies.

"Well, I can't eat muffins in an agitated manner. The butter would probably get on my cuffs. One should always eat muffins quite calmly. It is the only way to eat them." – Oscar Wilde; Algernon in *The Importance of Being Ernest*

## Potato Chip Eggs

A yummy way to put chips to use after their crisp has crusped.

*Serves: 2*

*Ingredients:*
2 eggs, beaten
1 c. potato chips
½ medium onion, finely chopped
olive oil
salt & pepper, hot sauce

*Preparation:*
1. Sauté the onions in 1 T. olive oil until soft.
2. Add a layer of potato chips on top of the onions. Do not mix them.
3. Pour the beaten eggs on top of the chips. Tilt the skillet to evenly coat the pan with eggs.
4. Cover and cook for about 2 minutes.
5. Divide into 2 servings and turn onto plates.
6. Serve with salt & pepper and hot sauce.
7. This is also nice with a sprinkle of fresh cilantro or parsley.

"I have many memories of waking up to eat breakfast that my mother carefully prepared for us and her saying, what do y'all want for lunch, and as we're eating lunch, what do y'all want for dinner? It's always about the next meal." – Lisa Loeb

## Biscuits, Eggs and Gravy

Biscuits and Gravy: Like licking the floor of heaven.

*Serves: 4*

*Ingredients:*
4 eggs
4 slices ham, sausage patties or links, or strips of bacon
4 slices American cheese
1 tube refrigerated biscuit dough
salt and pepper, hot sauce and catsup
aluminum pie pan
aluminum foil

*Preparation:*
1. Pull the biscuits off the tube and place them in a well-buttered aluminum pie pan. Cover the pan with foil and "bake" the biscuits on the grill or in the coals. Keep an eye on them.
2. Fry up the ham in a skillet with a little butter, and set it aside.
3. Fry the eggs in the ham juice with a little added butter if necessary, and melt a slice of cheese on each egg after you flip them.
4. Cut the biscuits in half. Put 1 egg 'n' cheese on each biscuit, top it with a slice of ham and the other half of the biscuit.
5. Serve with gravy. (See recipes below.) Or serve with salt and pepper, hot sauce and catsup.

"Powdermilk biscuits: Heavens, they're tasty and expeditious! They're made from whole wheat, to give shy persons the strength to get up and do what needs to be done" – Garrison Keillor

## Sausage Gravy

Name one thing that's better than gravy.

*Serves:* 4

*Ingredients:*
2 c. milk
3 T. white flour
butter
10 fatty breakfast sausages

*Preparation:*
1. Cook the sausages and set aside.
2. You need about 3 T. of sausage fat and juice. Make up any lacking with butter or olive oil.
3. Simmer the fat and slowly sprinkle in the flour, stirring vigorously with a fork the whole time, to make a paste.
4. Slowly add the milk, stirring vigorously with a fork the whole time. Stir and simmer until the gravy is thickened and the flour is cooked (it will taste browned, not like raw flour, when it's done).
5. Serve the gravy over biscuits with eggs and sausages. Or just eat it with a spoon.

*Variations:*
- Slice the sausages and add them back into the skillet when the gravy is cooked, and then pour the whole mess over biscuits.
- You can make this with bacon, but it's too greasy for me.

*TIP:*
- This doesn't usually need any seasoning because the sausages are well-seasoned.

"I come from a family where gravy is considered a beverage." – Erma Bombeck

## Vegetarian Sausage Gravy

A satisfying vegetarian version that everyone likes.

*Serves: 4*

*Ingredients:*
2 c. milk (for vegan gravy, use soy or nut milk)
3 T. white flour
olive oil
6 vegetarian breakfast sausage links

*Preparation:*
1. Cook the sausages gently in 2 T. of olive oil, so they release their juice and flavor. Remove the sausages and set aside.
2. You need about 3 T. of sausage juice and oil. Make up any lacking with olive oil.
3. Simmer the fat and slowly sprinkle in the flour, stirring vigorously with a fork the whole time, to make a paste.
4. Slowly add the milk, stirring with a fork the whole time. Stir and simmer until the gravy is thickened and the flour is cooked (it will taste browned, not like raw flour).
5. Serve with biscuits, eggs and the cooked sausage.

*Variation:*
- Make with vegetarian sausage patties and before you serve the gravy, add back the crumbled patties. Mmm.

"I didn't forget your breakfast. I didn't bring your breakfast. Because you didn't eat your din-din." – Bette Davis as Baby Jane Hudson in *Whatever Happened to Baby Jane*

## Breakfast Tacos

Kids like things wrapped in tortillas.

*Serves: 4*

*Ingredients:*
8 eggs, lightly beaten
6 patties breakfast sausage
½ small, yellow onion, chopped
¼ green pepper, chopped
4 oz. shredded cheese, such as Jack or Cheddar
1 small tomato, chopped
4 soft flour tortillas
salt & pepper, hot sauce and catsup

*Preparation:*
1. Crumble and cook the sausage in a skillet with the onion and green pepper.
2. Pour the eggs over the sausage and cook until set.
3. When the eggs are almost done, add the cheese and let it melt.
4. Spoon the eggs into warm tortillas, add chopped tomatoes, and roll them up.
5. Serve with salt & pepper, catsup and hot sauce.

*Variations:*
- Use salsa instead of chopped tomatoes.
- Use bacon, or link sausage, or ham, or chorizo for the grownups.
- Omit the eggs for a delicious sausage, tomato and cheese taco.
- Spread cream cheese on the tortillas before wrapping the burritos up.
- Add sautéed mushrooms.
- Add some thinly sliced green onions (scallions), sautéed or raw.
- Add black beans.
- Add leftover, cooked potatoes.

"I have met a lot of hardboiled eggs in my time, but you're twenty minutes."
– Oscar Wilde

## Huevos Rancheros

This is how we like them.

*Serves: 2*

*Ingredients:*
2 corn tortillas
2 eggs
olive oil
½ small, white onion, chopped
1 small tomato, chopped
1 medium handful cilantro (well washed), chopped
½ t. salt
4 oz. shredded cheese, like Jack or Mozzarella
salt & pepper and hot sauce

*Preparation:*
1. Chop the onion, tomato and cilantro and mix it with the salt to make Pico de Gallo.
2. Fry the eggs in a little olive oil.
3. Warm the tortillas and stack them. If the campfire isn't going yet, I warm the tortillas by balancing them on the frying pan while I'm cooking the eggs. But Pete does this by heating them directly on the camp stove burners. (Mmm, propane!)
4. Put the tortillas on plates.
5. Slide the eggs onto the tortillas.
6. Top with shredded cheese and Pico de Gallo.
7. Serve with salt & pepper, hot sauce and any leftover Pico de Gallo.

*Variations:*
- Some people hate cilantro, in which case, omit.
- Add some black beans if you have the consensus to open a can.

*TIP:*
- Wash and dry your veggies at home before you hit the road. Then you will have nice, clean cilantro to chop up for this dish.

"If more of us valued food and cheer and song above hoarded gold, it would be a merrier world." – J. R. R. Tolkien

## Eggs and Tortillas

A yummy way to use up the last couple of tortillas that are a little dried out.

*Serves: 4*

*Ingredients:*
6 eggs, lightly beaten
2 corn tortillas
butter
½ small, yellow onion, chopped
¼ green pepper, chopped
4 oz. shredded cheese, such as Jack or Mozzarella
salt & pepper, hot sauce and salsa

*Preparation:*
1. Sauté the onions and peppers in butter or oil until they're soft.
2. Tear the tortillas into little pieces and add them to the skillet. Cook them just until they start to brown.
3. Add the eggs and stir frequently as they cook.
4. Remove the pan from the heat and sprinkle with cheese.
5. Serve with salt & pepper, hot sauce and salsa.

"All happiness depends on a leisurely breakfast." – John Gunther

## Spam and Eggs

There is nothing equal to the joy of Spam and Eggs on day 5 of camping when all the fresh meat has been used up. And if you don't use it on one camping trip, you can always save it for the next one – it keeps!

*Serves: 4*

*Ingredients:*
8 eggs, lightly beaten
8 oz. Spam, diced
½ small, yellow onion chopped
¼ each red and green pepper, chopped
butter
salt & pepper, hot sauce, catsup and salsa

*Preparation:*
1. Sauté the onions, peppers and Spam until the Spam is browned and a little crispy.
2. Add the eggs and scramble it all together. Cook the eggs until they're done.
3. Serve with salt & pepper, hot sauce, catsup and salsa.

"Never work before breakfast; if you have to work before breakfast, eat your breakfast first." – Josh Billings

## Corned Beef Hash and Eggs

Just what is corned beef hash? It's beef, onions, potatoes and a whole lotta fat, overcooked and mashed together to make a delicious, gut-busting glop. Yummy.

*Serves: 2*

*Ingredients:*
½ can corned beef hash
4 eggs
2 slices American cheese
salt & pepper, hot sauce, salsa, spicy yellow mustard and A1 sauce

*Preparation:*
1. Warm ½ can corned beef hash in a skillet, stirring it occasionally.
2. Break the eggs onto the hash.
3. Lay the cheese on top of the eggs.
4. Cover the skillet and cook through, melting the cheese.
5. Serve with salt & pepper, salsa, hot sauce, spicy yellow mustard and A1 sauce.
6. Don't think about your arteries, they're fine.

*Variations:*
- Warm the corned beef hash in its own can on the fire – just remember to open it first. Learned that the hard way.
- Leftover corned beef hash is best eaten right away, right out of the can, on the sly.

"One of the very nicest things about life is the way we must regularly stop whatever it is we are doing and devote our attention to eating." – Luciano Pavarotti

## Eggs and Grits

We love grits, even without the bacon, eggs and cheese.

*Serves: 4*

*Ingredients:*
4 eggs, lightly beaten
4 strips bacon
4 packets instant grits*
8 oz. shredded cheese, such as Jack or Cheddar
salt & pepper and hot sauce

*Preparation:*
1. Fry the bacon in a skillet, and tear it into small pieces.
2. Boil some water for the grits (we bring a teakettle but a small pot is fine).
3. Empty the instant grits into 4 bowls. Add hot water per the directions on the box and stir.
4. Scramble the eggs in the bacon fat with the cooked bacon pieces. Don't cook the eggs too hard; they should be pretty soft.
5. Stir a spoonful of cooked eggs and bacon and a healthy sprinkle of shredded cheese into each bowl of grits.
6. Serve with salt and pepper and hot sauce.

*TIP:*
- *You can use real grits, but instant grits mean you don't have to clean the pot.

"Polenta? Oh, you mean Italian grits?" – Anonymous

## Rice Omelet

Good for using up any leftover rice from dinner.

*Serves: 4*

*Ingredients:*
1 c. of leftover cooked rice – white or brown
4 eggs, lightly beaten
4 strips bacon
½ small, yellow onion, chopped
½ green pepper, chopped
½ stalk of celery, chopped
1 small tomato, chopped
salt and pepper, hot sauce and catsup

*Preparation:*
1. Cook the bacon, tear it into small pieces and set it aside.
2. Cook the onion, pepper and celery in the bacon fat until nice and soft.
3. Add the tomato, the rice and add back the bacon, and stir well.
4. Add the eggs and let them set, then stir once and let them set again.
5. Serve with salt and pepper, hot sauce and catsup.

*Variation:*
- Use leftover noodles instead of rice.

"Rice is great if you're really hungry and you want to eat two thousand of something." – Mitch Hedber

## Rice and Eggs

Our kids like rice, so we often put on a pot for dinner, and we never throw out the leftovers. Here's a variation on the rice omelet.

*Serves: 4*

*Ingredients:*
4 eggs
4 strips bacon
½ medium onion, chopped
¼ green pepper, chopped
3 c. leftover cooked rice (white or brown)
1 handful cilantro, well washed and chopped (wash it at home)
butter or olive oil
salt and pepper, hot sauce and catsup

*Preparation:*
1. Chop the bacon and fry it in a skillet. Remove the bacon and drain it on a paper towel, leaving the bacon fat in the pan.
2. Wipe out all but 2 t. of the bacon fat with a paper towel. Add a little butter or olive oil and sauté the chopped onion and green pepper until soft.
3. Add the rice and bacon and heat through.
4. Move the rice to the sides of the pan and fry the eggs one by one in the center of the pan.
5. As each egg is fried, scoop up a spoonful of rice and put it on the plate, then add the egg on top.
6. Add a sprinkle of cilantro and serve with hot sauce, salt & pepper.
7. Ah, cilantro.

"Same old slippers, same old rice, same old glimpse of paradise." – William James Lampton

**Egg Bake in a Dutch Oven**

Dutch Ovens are good for big groups because then everyone can eat at the same time. We also like the Dutch Oven because you can put the food in the fire and do something else while it's cooking.

*Serves: 4*

*Ingredients:*
2 potatoes, sliced or 4 handfuls frozen hash browns
8 sausage links or 8 strips of bacon
8 eggs, lightly beaten
¾ lb. shredded cheese, such as Jack or Cheddar
olive oil or spray oil

*Preparation:*
1. Spray the bottom and sides of the Dutch Oven with cooking spray, or grease it with olive oil and a paper towel.
2. Put the sausage links or bacon on the bottom of the Dutch Oven.
3. Put the potato slices or hash browns on the sausage.
4. Add the eggs, sprinkle the whole thing with cheese and secure the lid tightly. Set it on hot coals and shovel hot coals on top of it.
5. Cook for around 20 minutes.

*Variations:*
- Add sliced mushrooms, chopped green or red pepper or any other veggies you like.
- Beat some cream or half 'n' half into the eggs for a richer flavor.
- Add seasoned breadcrumbs or crushed crackers on top, like Ritz crackers.

*TIP:*
- Check the Dutch Oven as often as you like. That's what barbecue tongs, a camping shovel and oven mitts are for. Besides, it's fun.

"Part of the secret success in life is to eat what you like and let the food fight it out inside." – Mark Twain

## Egg and Potato Packets

Everything tastes better when it's cooked in aluminum foil over an open fire.

*Serves: 1*

*Ingredients:*
1 egg
1 small handful frozen hash browns or chopped cooked potatoes.
2 strips bacon or 1 sausage patty
olive oil
salt & pepper, hot sauce and catsup
aluminum foil
paper towels

*Preparation:*
1. Tear off a rectangle of aluminum foil and fold it in half to make a double thick square.
2. Grease the foil with olive oil.
3. Put the sausage patty or bacon on the foil.
4. Put the hash browns or potatoes on top of the sausage.
5. Break an egg on top of the hash browns.
6. Wrap up the foil packet so the contents are snugly wrapped, but not too tight. Bend the ends of the packet to make handles for picking it up.
7. Place the packet directly on medium coals or on the hot part of the grill.
8. Serve with salt & pepper, hot sauce and catsup.

*Variations:*
- Add cheese.
- Add chopped tomatoes and onions.

"A food is not necessarily essential just because your child hates it."
– Katharine Whitehorn

## Sandwich Iron or Pie Iron Eggs (AKA in the olden days as Toas-Tites)

These are great for the kids to make for themselves in the campfire. Little kids need some help and supervision.

*Serves: 1*

*Ingredients:*
2 strips bacon cut in half to make 4 pieces
2 slices soft bread
1 egg

*Preparation:*
1. Put 2 pieces of bacon on one side of the sandwich iron. The bacon goes on the outside of the sandwich to grease the sandwich iron while it cooks.
2. Put a piece of bread on top of the bacon – push down the center to make a little nest for the egg.
3. Crack an egg into the nest.
4. Put another piece of bread on top of the egg.
5. Add 2 more pieces of bacon on top of the 2nd piece of bread.
6. Close the top of the sandwich iron, and latch it if it has a latch.
7. Put it over the hot coals for about 5 minutes, turning it several times.
8. Bon appétit!

Variations:
- Add cheese on top of the egg.
- Eliminate bacon by oiling the sandwich iron.
- Serve with salsa.

TIPS:
- You can cook the egg first if you want to. It's less messy.
- If you have a bunch of kids, you might want to get 2 sandwich irons.

"The fire is the main comfort of the camp, whether in summer or winter, and is about as ample at one season as at another. It is as well for cheerfulness as for warmth and dryness." – Henry David Thoreau

## Egg in an Orange

This is another classic for the kids and somewhat of an acquired taste. It's like eating the orange garnish off your plate when you order an omelet in a diner.

*Serves: 1*

*Ingredients:*
1 orange
1 egg
a knife and a spoon
salt & pepper

*Preparation:*
1. Cut the orange in half and scoop out (and eat) the orange with a spoon.
2. Scrape out all the white part inside the orange to make a perfect cup.
3. Break an egg into the orange cup.
4. Place the orange on the grill or perched in medium hot coals and cook for about 5 minutes.
5. Eat the egg out of the orange. (No dishes!)

*Variation:*
- Use a cooked potato or a raw onion instead of an orange. Scoop out the insides, break an egg into the center, wrap it in foil and cook it directly on the hot coals.

"A man is not an orange. You can't eat the fruit and throw the peel away."
– Arthur Miller

## Muffin eggs

This is a fun way to make eggs for everybody at the same time.

*Serves: 6*

*Ingredients:*
6 eggs
2 strips bacon
muffin tin

*Preparation:*
1. Cut each strip of bacon into 3 pieces, making 6 pieces total.
2. Put a piece of bacon into each of 6 muffin tin cups.
3. Place the muffin tin on the fire and cook the bacon until it's done to your liking.
4. Crack an egg into each cup on top of the bacon and cook until the eggs are done.

*Variation:*
- It's been said that all of my recipes contain bacon! Not true! Instead of bacon, you can cook the eggs in butter or olive oil.

"When you're in my house you shall do as I do and believe who I believe in. So Bart, butter your bacon." – Homer Simpson

# FRENCH TOAST AND PANCAKES

### Pie Iron Banana French Toast

It's fun to make anything in a pie iron. Don't forget the maple syrup!

*Serves:* 4

*Ingredients:*
4 slices bread
2 eggs
¼ c. milk
1 banana, sliced
maple syrup
butter

*Preparation:*
1. Heat the pie iron in the fire.
2. Spray the inside of the pie iron with cooking spray or rub both sides with a stick of butter.
3. Beat the eggs and milk together.
4. Dip one slice of bread in egg mixture and place on one side of the pie iron.
5. Put the sliced bananas on the bread.
6. Dip a second slice of bread and place it on top of the bananas.
7. Close the pie iron and cook it in the hot coals until the French toast is brown.
8. Serve with butter and maple syrup.

*Variation:*
- My kids like this with chopped apple in the center instead of banana. You can also add chocolate chips, peanut butter or a marshmallow.

"I went to a restaurant that serves 'breakfast at any time'. So I ordered French Toast during the Renaissance." – Steven Wright.

**Cake French Toast**

This is good for leftover Monkey Bread.

*Serves: 4*

*Ingredients:*
4 slices leftover cake, sweet rolls or Monkey Bread
2 eggs
¼ c. milk
butter

*Preparation:*
1. Beat the eggs with the milk.
2. Slice the leftover cake or sweet rolls.
3. Dip the cake into the egg mixture.
4. Fry in butter.
5. Serve with extra butter. Maple syrup isn't necessary because the cake is already so sweet.

"Man does not live by bread alone, even pre-sliced bread." – D. W. Brogan

## Hot Dog Bun French Toast

This recipe calls for more eggs than your average French toast because the rolls really sop up the egg mixture.

*Serves: 4*

*Ingredients:*
4 leftover hot dog rolls or hamburger rolls
butter
3 eggs
½ c. milk
cinnamon
maple syrup

*Preparation:*
1. Beat the eggs and milk in a large bowl.
2. Heat the skillet with 1 T. of butter.
3. Break the rolls into little pieces and dump all of the pieces into the egg mixture. Stir it around and pour the whole thing into a large skillet (you may need to cook this in batches, depending on the size of your skillet).
4. Sprinkle the top with cinnamon.
5. Cook it 2 or 3 minutes until it's browned on the bottom, then flip the whole thing over.
6. Cook another 2 or 3 minutes, until the egg and bread are cooked through.
7. Serve with butter and maple syrup.

*Variation:*
- This is also great with a small can of cling peaches, drained and chopped – just mix it in before you dump it in the pan.

"'When you wake up in the morning, Pooh,' said Piglet at last, 'what's the first thing you say to yourself?' 'What's for breakfast?' said Pooh. 'What do you say, Piglet?' 'I say, I wonder what's going to happen exciting today?' said Piglet. Pooh nodded thoughtfully. 'It's the same thing,' he said." – A. A. Milne, *The House at Pooh Corner*

## Apple Pancakes

We make pancakes from scratch when we go camping, because we do it so often at home that we're used to it. But feel free to bring instant pancake mix or even the kind you squirt out of a jug.

*Serves: 4*

*Ingredients:*
2 c. whole wheat flour
2 T. sugar
2 t. baking soda
a pinch of salt
1 egg
2 c. milk
1 apple, peeled, cored and chopped fine
butter
maple syrup

*Preparation:*
1. Mix the dry ingredients in a bowl.
2. Make a well in the middle of the dry ingredients and beat the egg in it.
3. Mix in the milk bit by bit in the well until you have the right consistency. It should be thicker than drippy but not so thick that it's ploppy.
4. Mix in the apple.
5. Let it sit for 5-10 minutes.
6. Butter the skillet.
7. Bring the skillet to perfect heat – the butter should be hot but not smoking.
8. Allow for your first pancake to be a dud.
9. Your second pancake should be nice and brown and crispy on the outside and cooked through. You flip it when it bubbles on top.
10. Serve with butter and maple syrup.

*Tips:*
- If you have a campfire going, you can cook the pancakes on the lid of your Dutch Oven. Put the lid upside down on the coals and spray with cooking oil. Use it like a griddle.
- Leftover, cooked pancakes make nice snacks.

"Cooking is an art, but you eat it too." – Marcella Hazan

# FRUIT AND CEREAL

**Campfire Applesauce**

The perfect Dutch Oven recipe – let it bubble away in the fire while you make dinner.

*Serves: 4*

*Ingredients:*
8 apples, peeled, cored and cut into quarters or eighths
1/3 c. brown sugar
2 T. cornstarch (you can skip this, but your sauce will take longer to thicken)
½ t. salt
1 T. cinnamon
4 T. butter

*Preparation:*
1. Warm up the Dutch Oven in the fire.
2. Peel, core and cut the apples.
3. Put all of the ingredients except the butter into the Dutch Oven and stir.
4. Dot with butter.
5. Cover and cook 30 minutes or until the apples are soft and the sauce is thick. Use a shovel to cover the Dutch Oven with hot coals.

"I know the look of an apple that is roasting and sizzling on the hearth on a winter's evening, and I know the comfort that comes of eating it hot, along with some sugar and a drench of cream ... I know how the nuts taken in conjunction with winter apples, cider, and doughnuts, make old people's tales and old jokes sound fresh and crisp and enchanting." – Mark Twain

## Wormy Apple

Don't use a real worm.

*Serves: 1*

*Ingredients:*
1 apple
1 precooked sausage link
aluminum foil
an apple corer

*Preparation:*
1. Core the apple.
2. Poke the sausage link through the apple – that's the worm.
3. Wrap the apple in foil.
4. Cook it on medium coals 15-30 minutes, until the apple is soft and yummy.

*Variations:*
- Sprinkle with cinnamon or brown sugar.
- Serve with maple syrup.

"If worms carried pistols, birds wouldn't eat 'em." – Darrell Royal

## Fruit and Yogurt Parfait

One of my kids loves yogurt, so I always bring a couple of containers along. When everyone else is gobbling up bacon and eggs, I make her this special treat.

*Serves: 1*

*Ingredients:*
1 8 oz. container yogurt (we like vanilla)
½ apple, chopped
1 handful grapes, halved
1 box raisins
1 handful granola
a clear plastic cup

*Preparation:*
1. Layer the fruit, yogurt and granola in the plastic cup. Make it pretty.
2. Serve with a festive spoon.

"A table, a chair, a bowl of fruit and a violin; what else does a man need to be happy?" – Albert Einstein

## Banana Taco

This is nice for kids who like a cold breakfast, or for morning wanderers who like brekkie on the run.

*Serves: 1*

*Ingredients:*
1 soft flour tortilla
1 banana
peanut butter

*Preparation:*
1. Spread the tortilla with peanut butter.
2. Peel the banana and place it on top of the peanut butter in the tortilla.
3. Roll it up.
4. Buen Provecho!

*Variation:*
- This is also yummy with Nutella.

"Never interrupt me when I'm eating a banana." – Ryan Stiles

### Granola (make at home)

Granola is a lot cheaper to make than it is to buy, and the kids enjoy making it. This is a basic recipe; you can put anything you like in granola, just start with oats.

*Serves: 8*

*Ingredients:*
4 c. extra thick oats
¼ c. walnut pieces
¼ c. almond slices
¼ c. sunflower seeds
2 t. ground cinnamon
1 t. orange zest or minced orange peel (just the orange part)
1 t. vanilla extract
½ c. honey
1 stick butter, melted
½ c. Craisins (dried, sweetened cranberries) or raisins

*Preparation:*
1. Preheat the oven to 300 degrees.
2. Combine everything except the Craisins with your clean hands in a big bowl.
3. Spread the granola out on a big, flat jellyroll pan (a cookie sheet with a lip). Bake for 45 minutes, stirring regularly, until it's crunchy.
4. Remove from the oven and stir in the cranberries.
5. Cool the granola completely before packing or it will be one big chunk of granola.

*Variation:*
- Add wheat germ, coconut or any other dried fruit or nuts.

"If wishes and buts were clusters of nuts, we'd all have a bowl of granola."
– from *Strangers with Candy* (don't let your kids watch this show.)

**A Word about Hot Cereals**

1. Wheatina. When I was a kid and went camping, we had Wheatina for breakfast every morning. Wheatina is an extremely bland, earthy-flavored, hot cereal. Every time I taste it it reminds me of camping, but I make it a point to not taste it very often. Go ahead and try it for yourself. My father liked it enough to cook it at home, but I can't imagine why.

2. Grits. Love 'em! Kind of messy to clean up, so I would recommend the instant kind for camping. Don't need a recipe for that.

3. Oatmeal. See above. Use instant.

"Like religion, politics, and family planning, cereal is not a topic to be brought up in public. It's too controversial." – Erma Bombeck

MAGGIE DA SILVA

# SOUPS, SIDES, STARTERS AND SNACKS

*Homemade fire starters*

MAGGIE DA SILVA

# SOUPS AND SIDES

**Clam Chowder**

This is the only soup we ever make when we go camping. We use low-sodium chicken broth because the clam juice and the bacon are already salty, and I like whole milk instead of cream.

*Serves: 4*

*Ingredients:*
8 slices bacon
1 10 oz. jar or can chopped clams, including the juice
1 8 oz. bottle clam juice
2 c. low-sodium chicken broth
2 c. milk
1 small yellow onion, chopped
2 medium potatoes, chopped
2 carrots, peeled and sliced
1 c. canned or frozen corn or 2 ears of fresh corn, broken in half
1 bay leaf
½ t. of thyme
butter
salt & pepper

*Preparation:*
1. Cook the bacon in a big pot. Remove and reserve the bacon and leave about 2 T. of bacon fat in the pot. If there isn't enough, add some butter to make 2 T.
2. Sauté the onions in the bacon fat until they are soft but not browned.
3. Add the potatoes and sauté for just a minute or two, until everything is nicely blended together.
4. If you want a thicker chowder, you can sprinkle in 1 T. of white flour at this point and mix it all together until everything is coated evenly with flour.
5. Add the bottle of clam juice, the juice from the jar or can of clams, the chicken broth, the carrots, the bay leaf and the thyme.
6. Simmer for 20 minutes, or until the potatoes are tender.
7. Add the corn and simmer for another 2 minutes.
8. Add the clams and the milk, and season carefully with salt and pepper – don't let it get too salty.
9. Heat the soup until it's steaming hot, but don't let it boil. Put a pat of butter on top while it's heating up.

10. Serve with crumbled bacon on top, oyster crackers (or hard tack!) and salt & pepper.

*Variations:*
- Add fresh fish filets, canned crab, peeled and cleaned shrimp or any other kind of seafood.
- Omit the seafood and add extra corn and potatoes for corn chowder.
- Substitute chicken or beef broth for the milk. This makes a chowder like one we often have in Rhode Island, which tastes like it's made from sea water. (It probably is, and we love it.)
- Add frozen peas.
- Use fresh clams (what a concept!). Scrub them well and steam them in a big pot. Only use the ones that open (chopped) and use the cooking water from the clams (with the sand strained out) instead of some of the clam juice, depending on how flavorful the water is.

"But when that smoking chowder came in, the mystery was delightfully explained. Oh! Sweet friends, hearken to me. It was made of small juicy clams, scarcely bigger than hazel nuts, mixed with pounded ship biscuits and salted pork cut up into little flakes! The whole enriched with butter, and plentifully seasoned with pepper and salt.....we dispatched it with great expedition." – Herman Melville, Ishmael in *Moby Dick*

## Baked Potato

The original campfire food. Here's the basic how-to with some delightful variations.

*Serves: 1*

*Ingredients:*
1 large potato, scrubbed clean
olive oil
salt & pepper, butter and sour cream
aluminum foil

*Preparation:*
1. Poke the potato with a fork in several places.
2. Coat the potato in olive oil.
3. Wrap the potato tightly in a double thickness of foil and place it on the hot coals for about 30 minutes. (Check it with a fork or skewer.)
4. Serve the potato with salt & pepper, butter and sour cream.

*Variations:*
- Substitute bacon fat for the olive oil, or wrap the potato in a strip of bacon.
- Slice a potato and an onion and alternate the slices together. Add a drizzle of olive oil and a sprinkle of salt and pepper, wrap it up in foil and cook it on the coals.
- Try different seasonings, like garlic salt or seasoned salt like Lawry's.
- I've heard of campers packing their baked potatoes in a ball of mud and cooking it that way in the coals! We've never done that but it sounds like fun.

*TIPS:*
- Check your potato from time to time; don't let it turn into ashes.
- You can cut the potato in half and cook each half separately to save time.

"For me, a plain baked potato is the most delicious one....It is soothing and enough." – M.F.K. Fisher

## Dutch Oven Potatoes and Bacon

A great side dish – you set it in the coals and when it's almost done, start your steaks on the grill. Perfect.

*Serves: 4*

*Ingredients:*
4 large potatoes, sliced
1 large, yellow onion, quartered
8 strips bacon, chopped
sour cream
salt & pepper

*Preparation:*
1. Chop the bacon and put it on the bottom of the Dutch Oven.
2. Break apart the onion quarters and lay the pieces on top of the bacon.
3. Slice the potatoes and spread them over the onions.
4. Season everything with salt & pepper.
5. Cover the Dutch Oven, set it on the hot coals and shovel some hot coals on top of the Dutch Oven.
6. Cook for about 40 minutes, checking every 15 minutes or so.
7. Serve with salt & pepper and sour cream.

*Variations:*
- Add shredded cheese on top.
- Add frozen green peas.

"What I say is that, if a fellow really likes potatoes, he must be a pretty decent sort of fellow." – A. A. Milne

## Potato and Veggie Foil Packets

We make these every time we go camping to trick our kids into eating vegetables.

*Serves: 4*

*Ingredients:*
4 small potatoes, chopped
2 carrots, peeled and sliced
½ each green and red pepper, sliced
8 oz. cheese, such as Jack, Cheddar or Velveeta, shredded
butter
salt & pepper, hot sauce and sour cream

*Preparation:*
1. Tear off 4 rectangles of aluminum foil and fold them in half to make double thick squares.
2. Grease the foil with olive oil, butter or spray oil.
3. Let the kids assemble their own packets with the onions, carrots and peppers. Season them with salt & pepper.
4. Put a pat of butter on top of each, and let the kids add the shredded cheese.
5. Wrap up the foil packets so the contents are snugly wrapped, but not too tight. Bend the ends of the packets to make handles for picking them up.
6. Place the packets directly on medium coals or on the hot part of the grill.
7. Turn them every 5 minutes or so, and cook them for about 20 minutes, or until everything is cooked through.
8. Serve with salt & pepper, hot sauce and sour cream.

*Variations:*
- You can omit the veggies and just make potato packets, or visa-versa.
- Try different veggies, like baby carrots, broccoli florets, mushrooms, cabbage, baby red potatoes or yellow or green squash.
- Add scallions or fresh garlic.
- Add a strip of rare-cooked bacon to the bottom of the packet, under the onions, or a dab of bacon grease for flavor.
- Try different seasonings with this, like fresh rosemary, chili powder, seasoned salt like Lawry's, garlic salt or powder or onion soup mix.
- Try marinating the veggies in salad dressing before cooking.

*TIP:*
- When making this for a group, put everything in an aluminum pan and

cover it with foil. (Or use a Dutch Oven.) Cook it on a hot grill or in the coals for about 45 minutes, stirring every 5 or 10 minutes.

"Potatoes served at breakfast, At dinner served again; Potatoes served at supper, Forever and Amen!" – Pennsylvania prayer

*Foil Packets on the grill*

## Roasted Potatoes

Potatoes for a group. Multiply as needed.

*Serves: 4*

*Ingredients:*
4 large potatoes, cubed
1 glove garlic, minced
olive oil
butter
salt & pepper, hot sauce, catsup and A1 sauce
aluminum foil pan
aluminum foil

*Preparation:*
1. Grease the aluminum pan with olive oil.
2. Add the potatoes to the pan and sprinkle with the minced garlic.
3. Drizzle the potatoes with olive oil and season with salt & pepper.
4. Mix them up with a big spoon, turning them over until the garlic is mixed in.
5. Cover the pan with foil and set it on the hot grill or in the coals.
6. Cook the potatoes about 30 minutes, stirring occasionally. Add more oil if needed.

*Variations:*
- Use baby red potatoes.
- Use fresh rosemary, garlic salt or powder, lemon pepper or Lawrey's seasoned salt.
- Add chopped onions.
- Sprinkle with Parmesan or another cheese.
- Sprinkle with powdered ranch dressing (you heard me) or onion soup mix.
- Add a small can of sliced black olives.

"My idea of heaven is a great big baked potato and someone to share it with."
– Oprah Winfrey

## Catsup Potatoes

When kids hear the word 'catsup', they figure dinner might be edible. But this is actually nice with steak for the grownups.

*Serves: 4*

*Ingredients:*
3 leftover baked potatoes, cubed
1 small clove garlic, minced
½ small, yellow onion, chopped
¼ green pepper, chopped
olive oil
catsup
salt & pepper

*Preparation:*
1. Sauté the onion, green pepper and garlic in 1 T. of olive oil, being careful to not burn the garlic.
2. Add 1 more T. of olive oil and ¼ c. of catsup and mix well.
3. Add the potatoes and mix carefully to combine – you don't want to end up with mashed potatoes.
4. Cook the potatoes until they're heated through, about 5 minutes. Add more catsup or oil if necessary.
5. Serve with salt & pepper.

*TIP:*
- For a big group, pre-bake a bunch of potatoes at home. This is a good idea anyway, so hungry little campers can have a baked potato *tout suite*.

"Eat, drink, and be merry, for tomorrow we may diet." – Harry Kurnitz

## Twice-Baked Potatoes

Great for leftover baked potatoes.

*Serves: 4*

*Ingredients:*
4 large potatoes, baked
2 T. butter
½ c. cheddar cheese, grated or shredded
¼ c. milk, sour cream or even plain yogurt
salt & pepper
aluminum foil

*Preparation:*
1. Bake potatoes at home or in the campfire coals. They take about an hour in the coals - and watch them carefully so they don't overcook and turn to ashes!
2. After they cool, slice each potato down the middle (not all the way through) and scoop out the insides into a bowl, reserving the skins.
3. Mash the potato insides with the butter and milk. Season with salt and pepper and mix in the cheese.
4. Scoop the potato mixture back into the skins. Place side by side in a skillet and cover with foil.
5. Cook on the grill until the cheese melts, 10-15 minutes.

*TIP:*
- We often bake potatoes at home and bring them with us, to ensure we get edible baked potatoes.

"Is that weird, taking my Louis Vuitton bag camping?" – Jessica Simpson

## French Fries

When a dark cloud of grumpiness descends, French fries bring back the sunshine.

*Serves: 4*

*Ingredients:*
3 potatoes
olive oil
salt & pepper
garlic powder or other spices
aluminum foil

*Preparation:*
1. Cut the potatoes into ½" thick sticks.
2. Tear off a large piece of aluminum foil and spread olive oil on it.
3. Lay the fries in a single layer on the aluminum foil and sprinkle with salt & pepper and any other spices you like.
4. Cover with a 2nd piece of foil and lay the whole thing on the campfire grill.
5. Check it from time to time and turn the fries. I use a wooden spoon so it doesn't puncture the foil like a metal spatula does.
6. Cook for about 30 minutes.

*TIPS:*
- Purists deride the use of garlic powder. Purists also have fingers that smell like garlic the whole camping trip!
- A jelly roll pan (a cookie sheet with a lip) would be the ideal cooking pan in this case, but we never remember to bring one. Maybe you will.

"French fries. I love them. Some people are chocolate and sweets people. I love French fries. That and caviar." – Cameron Diaz

## Scalloped Potatoes

This is a good Dutch Oven recipe, but we have done it many times with just an aluminum foil baking pan, too. Great for leftover baked potatoes.

*Serves: 4*

*Ingredients:*
3 large potatoes, sliced thin
1 medium onion, sliced thin
8 oz. Jack or other cheese, grated
1 pint milk
olive oil
butter, 1 stick+
salt & pepper
aluminum foil
baking pan

*Preparation:*
1. Spread olive oil on inside of your baking pan.
2. Spread a layer of potato slices on the bottom of the pan, add a layer of onion, dot with butter and sprinkle with cheese.
3. Repeat the layers until all the potatoes and onions are used up.
4. Dot the top with butter and sprinkle with salt and pepper.
5. Pour in milk to cover.
6. Cover tightly with aluminum foil and place in the coals of the fire, under the grill. Cook for about 45 minutes, checking often. You may need to add milk as you go to keep the potatoes from burning on the bottom.

*Variations:*
- Sprinkle with Parmesan cheese and breadcrumbs for Potatoes au Gratin.
- Add a layer of sliced or cubed ham.
- Serve with jalapenos!

*TIPS:*
- You can make a smaller or individual versions of this using aluminum pie pans. It's easier to maneuver the pie pans and they take up less space in the fire.

"Blessed are the cheesemakers." – Monty Python, *Life of Brian*

## Roasted Veggies

The grownups like these.

Serves: 6

Ingredients:
½ head broccoli, cut into florets and stem pieces (peel the stem first)
½ head cauliflower, cut into small chunks
¾ lb. asparagus, trimmed and cut in half
6 carrots, peeled and sliced
8 baby red potatoes, halved
1 red pepper, cored, seeded and sliced
2 cloves garlic, minced
olive oil
salt & pepper and hot sauce
aluminum foil pan
aluminum foil

Preparation:
1. Grease the aluminum pan well with olive oil.
2. Add all the veggies to the pan and drizzle with about ½ c. of olive oil.
3. Sprinkle the veggies with the garlic and mix everything well.
4. Cover the pan with foil and place it on the hot grill or in the coals.
5. Cook the veggies for about 45 minutes, mixing them every 15 minutes or so.
6. Serve with salt & pepper and hot sauce

"Cauliflower is nothing but cabbage with a college education." – Mark Twain

**Sautéed or Roasted Mushrooms**

We could eat about 5 pounds of mushrooms, as long as someone else would clean them. We often wash other veggies at home, but mushrooms keep a lot better in their original grit. So get the kids to help wash 'em at the campsite.

*Serves: 2*

*Ingredients:*
8 oz. mushrooms, washed and halved
olive oil
salt & pepper
foil pie plate or skillet
aluminum foil

*Preparation:*
1. Have a young child wash your mushrooms carefully, dipping them in a basin of water and gently rubbing away the grit.
2. Trim the ends off and discard.
3. Halve or slice the mushrooms, or leave them whole.
4. Place your mushrooms and about 2 T. of oil in the pie pan or skillet and sprinkle with salt and pepper.
5. Cover the skillet or pie pan with a cover or aluminum foil. Simmer on low for about 20 minutes.
6. Remove the cover or open the packet and simmer and additional 5-10 minutes, until all the liquid is evaporated.

"Not presume to dictate, but broiled fowl and mushrooms – capital thing!"
– Charles Dickens

## Stuffed Mushrooms

A simple way to add to the joy of mushrooms.

*Serves: 4*

*Ingredients:*
1 lb. large mushrooms
1 sausage patty, regular or meatless
3 T. prepared breadcrumbs
3 T. Parmesan cheese, grated olive oil aluminum foil baking pan aluminum foil

*Preparation:*
1. Have a young child wash your mushrooms carefully, dipping them in a basin of water and gently rubbing away the grit.
2. Trim the ends off and discard.
3. Carefully pull off the mushroom stems and chop them finely.
4. Cook the sausage patty in a skillet with a little olive oil, breaking it up into a ground meat consistency. Cool.
5. Mix about half a cup of the chopped mushroom stems, the crumbled sausage patty, breadcrumbs and Parmesan cheese together.
6. Stuff the caps with the mushroom/sausage mixture.
7. Spread about 1 T. of olive oil in the baking pan and arrange the mushroom caps in the pan. Cover the pan with foil.
8. Cook on the grill for about 10 minutes, then take the top off and cook another five minutes.
9. Be patient and don't burn your tongue!

"Nature alone is antique, and the oldest art a mushroom." – Thomas Carlyle

## Green Beans

*Serves: 4*

*Ingredients:*
1 lb. fresh green beans, washed
butter
salt & pepper

*Preparation:*
1. Snap the ends off the green beans.
2. Melt 1 T. butter in a skillet.
3. Cook the green beans in the butter until just tender, about 4 minutes.
4. Serve with salt & pepper.

*Variations:*
- Sprinkle some chopped, cooked bacon on top before serving.
- Squeeze with lemon before serving.

"Eat butter first, and eat it last, and live till a hundred years be past." – Old Dutch proverb

## Grilled Asparagus

*Serves: 4*

*Ingredients:*
1.5 lbs. asparagus with the bottoms snapped off
olive oil
salt & pepper
skewers

*Preparation:*
1. If you use wooden skewers, soak them in water first so they don't burn up on the grill.
2. Lay 4 or 5 asparagus spears down next to each other and skewer through all of them with 2 skewers. (Use 2 skewers so the spears don't spin around on one skewer.)
3. Repeat with all of the asparagus.
4. Brush the asparagus skewers with olive oil and lay them on the grill.
5. Sprinkle them with salt and pepper.
6. Grill until the asparagus is tender, 5-10 minutes, turning often.
7. Serve with salt & pepper.

"Asparagus inspires gentle thoughts." – Charles Lamb

## Corn on the Cob

A husks-on approach.

*Serves: 4*

*Ingredients:*
4 ears corn, with the husks on
butter
salt & pepper and hot sauce

*Preparation:*
1. Leaving the husks on, remove the floss or silk from each ear of corn.
2. Fold the husks back around the corn and submerge the corn in water to soak. After they have soaked for about 15 minutes, retrieve the corn from the water, wrap the husks around them more tightly, and place them on the grill, over medium heat, for 5-10 minutes.
3. Remove the husks and serve the corn with butter, salt & pepper and hot sauce.

*Variations:*
- You can also take the whole husk off before grilling and wrap each ear in foil spread with butter or cream cheese. These can go right on the coals, also.
- Try this with different spices, like Cajun seasoning.
- Try drizzling teriyaki sauce on the corn before you grill it.

*TIP:*
- We put the ears of corn in a big pot of water and hold them underwater with a skillet, but you can also place them in a plastic bag and hold it underwater with a rock, especially if you're camping near a stream.

"Plough deep, while Sluggards sleep; And you shall have Corn, to sell and to keep." – Benjamin Franklin, *Poor Richard's Almanac*

## Onion Flowers

*Serves: 1-2*

*Ingredients:*
1 large yellow or Vidalia onion
1 clove garlic
butter
salt & pepper

*Preparation:*
1. Slice the onion into quarters, but don't cut it all the way through, so the bottom of the onion is still attached.
2. Put a clove of garlic and a pat of butter in the center of the onion, and season it with salt & pepper.
3. Wrap the onion in aluminum foil and cook it on hot coals or on the grill for about 30 minutes.
4. Let it cool, and serve with salt & pepper.

*Variations:*
- Try this drizzled with Ranch dressing for the kids.
- Try it with garlic salt or powder instead of fresh garlic.
- Try it sprinkled with a little oregano.

"Happy is said to be the family which can eat onions together. They are, for the time being, separate, from the world, and have a harmony of aspiration."
– Charles Dudley Warner

## Zucchini Boats

Kids like to eat food shaped like vehicles, everyone knows that. This is also a good way to use up leftover rice.

*Serves: 4*

*Ingredients:*
2 large zucchini
½ medium onion, chopped
½ green pepper, chopped
1 stick of celery, chopped
1 c. mushrooms, chopped
1 small tomato, chopped
1 c. leftover cooked rice
1 egg
¼ c. prepared breadcrumbs
¼ c. Parmesan cheese, grated
olive oil
salt & pepper, hot sauce
aluminum foil baking pan
aluminum foil

*Preparation:*
1. Slice the zucchini lengthwise and scoop out enough insides to make a trough for the filling. Sprinkle the zucchini with salt and pepper.
2. Sauté the onions, pepper, celery, mushrooms and chopped tomato in 1 T. oil until soft. Cool.
3. Add the rice, Parmesan and breadcrumbs to the sautéed vegetables. Salt and pepper to taste.
4. Coat the baking pan with olive oil and place the zucchini boats inside.
5. Fill the boats with stuffing – it can be mounded up high. Cover the pan with aluminum foil and cook on the grill over the campfire for 30-45 minutes, until the zucchini is soft.
6. Serve with salt & pepper and hot sauce.

*Variation:*
- Add meat or tofu to turn this into a main dish.

"This cabbage, these carrots, these potatoes, these onions ... will soon become me. Such a tasty fact!" – Mike Garofalo

## Dutch Oven Sweet Potatoes and Apples

Kids love it, and it's good with pork chops.

*Serves: 4*

*Ingredients:*
4 Macintosh apples, peeled and sliced
3 large sweet potatoes, peeled and sliced
2 t. cinnamon
4 T. butter
1 c. apple juice or cider

*Preparation:*
1. Melt the butter in the bottom of a Dutch Oven.
2. Mix the sliced apples and sweet potatoes together with the cinnamon and apple juice.
3. Pour the mixture into the Dutch Oven.
4. Cover the Dutch Oven and put it on the coals for about 45 minutes.

"Surely the apple is the noblest of fruits." – Henry David Thoreau, *Wild Apples*

**Sweet, Sweet Potatoes**

The kids like these, and sweet potatoes are secretly very nutritious.

*Serves: 4*

*Ingredients:*
4 sweet potatoes
4 marshmallows (don't judge me!)
2 T. butter
4 t. brown sugar
salt
aluminum foil

*Preparation:*
1. Wash sweet potatoes thoroughly, wrap in aluminum foil and cook them in the coals of the fire for 30-45 minutes, checking often. (Or cook them at home, like we do!)
2. Chop the marshmallows.
3. Remove the potatoes from the fire, unwrap them and slice each one open lengthways.
4. Add a pat of butter to each potato, sprinkle with a brown sugar and chopped marshmallows and wrap the potatoes back up.
5. Place the potatoes back in the fire until the marshmallows melt, about 5 minutes.
6. Remove and cool. Serve with salt, to taste.

"My dream is to become a farmer. Just a Bohemian guy pulling up his own sweet potatoes for dinner." – Lenny Kravitz

## Mapley Sweet Potatoes

Diehard maple syrup fanatics like us always tote a jug of the good stuff with us.

*Serves: 4*

*Ingredients:*
4 sweet potatoes
6 T. butter
salt
maple syrup

*Preparation:*
1. Wash sweet potatoes thoroughly, wrap in aluminum foil and cook them in the coals of the fire for 30-45 minutes, checking often. (Or cook them at home, like we do!)
2. Remove the potatoes from the fire, scoop out the insides and mash with 4 T. of the butter. Season with salt, to taste.
3. As you serve the sweet potatoes, dot each serving with butter and let each person drizzle with maple syrup.

*Variation:*
- Use brown sugar instead of maple syrup.

"In contemplating the present opening prospects in human affairs, I am led to expect that a material part of the general happiness which heaven seems to have prepared for mankind, will be derived from the manufacture and general use of Maple Sugar." – Letter to Thomas Jefferson by Benjamin Rush, August 19, 1791

## Pink Salad

Kids like pink things. These veggies keep well in the cooler, so this is a good day 3 salad.

*Serves: 4*

*Ingredients:*
½ bag shredded carrots
½ bag shredded cabbage
½ c. dried cranberries
raspberry salad dressing – Trader Joe's has one

*Preparation:*
1. Mix the veggies and the cranberries together.
2. Dish into bowls and serve with salad dressing on the side so the kids can dress their own.

*Variation:*
- Serve with other dressing, such as soy-ginger, poppy seed, ranch or French.

"In the night the cabbages catch at the moon, the leaves drip silver, the rows of cabbages are a series of little silver waterfalls in the moon." – Carl Sandburg

## Bacon Salad

We call this bacon salad because then the kids forget it has vegetables in it.

*Serves: 4*

*Ingredients:*
¾ lb. green beans, with the ends snapped off
4 carrots, peeled and sliced
1 red pepper, sliced
4 oz. Parmesan cheese, shredded
4 strips bacon, cooked crisp

*Preparation:*
1. Put the veggies and cheese into a large pot or bowl.
2. Crumble the bacon in and toss the salad gently.
3. Serve with a creamy dressing, like Ranch.

*Variations:*
- Try with different veggies like cauliflower and broccoli.
- Try with other dressings, like soy-ginger, poppy seed or French.

"We don't need a melting pot in this country, folks. We need a salad bowl. In a salad bowl, you put in the different things. You want the vegetables - the lettuce, the cucumbers, the onions, the green peppers - to maintain their identity. You appreciate differences." – Jane Elliot

## Bread Salad (Panzanella)

This is a good day two salad, if you plan to have Italian bread at dinner on day one.

*Serves: 4*

*Ingredients:*
4 c. leftover Italian bread or Focaccia, cubed
1 large tomato, diced
1 cucumber, peeled and diced
½ yellow onion, sliced thinly
1 small clove garlic, minced
1 anchovy, chopped
½ c. fresh basil leaves
½ c. olive oil
juice of 1 lemon
salt & pepper

*Preparation:*
1. Make the salad dressing: Pour the olive oil and lemon juice into a jar with a screw top. Add the garlic and the anchovy and shake well. Salt and pepper to taste.
2. Put the cubed bread in a pot and drizzle with about half of the dressing. Toss it well to coat the bread.
3. Add the tomato, cucumber, onion and basil leaves and the rest of the salad dressing and toss gently.
4. Serve with salt & pepper. Eat the remaining anchovies on the sly.

"A loaf of bread, a jug of wine, and thou." – Omar Khayyam

## Nancy Nutter's Orzo Salad

This is the salad my mom makes all summer. Easy and delicious!

*Serves: 6-8*

*Ingredients:*
1 lb. orzo
4 oz. feta cheese, crumbled
1 small can sliced black olives
1 small jar marinated sundried tomatoes, chopped
salad dressing – my mom likes bottled "Greek-style", but you can use any oil and vinegar dressing
salt & pepper

*Preparation:*
1. Cook orzo in salted, boiling water according to the package directions. Drain.
2. Combine orzo, feta and sundried tomatoes.
3. Dress according to taste with salad dressing.
4. Opa!

*Variations:*
- Add chopped artichoke hearts, Greek olives, fresh tomatoes, chopped parsley or anything else that looks good.

"Tomatoes and oregano make it Italian; wine and tarragon make it French. Sour cream makes it Russian; lemon and cinnamon make it Greek. Soy sauce makes it Chinese; garlic makes it good." – Alice May Brock

## Rice and Beans

I would eat this every day, accompanied by a big bottle of hot sauce.

*Serves: 4*

*Ingredients:*
1 small yellow onion, chopped
1 stalk celery, chopped
¼ red and green pepper, chopped
1 can black beans
1 c. white rice
olive oil
3 c. chicken broth
salt & pepper and hot sauce

*Preparation:*
1. Sauté the onions, celery and peppers in 1 T. of olive oil until they're soft, about 5 minutes.
2. Mix in the beans and the rice.
3. Add the chicken broth and bring it to a simmer.
4. Cover the pot and simmer until the rice is cooked, about 15 minutes.
5. Serve with salt & pepper and hot sauce.

*Variations:*
- Add some leftover, cooked sausage or cooked, crumbled bacon.
- Mix in a couple of beaten eggs and cook through for fried rice and beans.
- Add a chopped tomato while the rice is simmering, or afterwards, on top.

"Red beans and ricely yours." – Louis Armstrong signed his personal correspondence this way.

# STARTERS

## Nachos

*Serves: 4*

*Ingredients:*
1 bag lightly salted tortilla ships (our kids complain the regular ones are too salty)
½ lb. ground beef or 4 links Italian sausages or both
1 lb. mild cheese, such as Jack, Velveeta or American
1 c. lettuce, shredded
1 tomato, chopped
1 avocado, sliced
a handful of green olives, sliced
salsa
sour cream
salt & pepper and hot sauce
aluminum pie plates
aluminum foil

*Preparation:*
1. Cook the hamburger and/or sausages until done. Season the hamburger with salt & pepper and slice the sausages.
2. Let each kid assemble their own individual nachos in a pie plate. Start with chips on the bottom, then layer on some meat and sprinkle the top with cheese.
3. Cover each pie plate with foil and heat them on the grill until the cheese melts.
4. Top each plate of nachos with a sprinkle of lettuce, tomato and olives, a few avocado slices and a dollop of sour cream. Leave the salsa out for extra dipping.
5. Serve with salt & pepper and hot sauce, and a fork!

*Variations:*
- Heat a can of black, red or refried beans on the grill for everyone who likes beans.
- Try with some canned corn – just pop open the can and heat it on the grill.
- Try with sliced scallions on top.
- Try cooking the beef with some chopped onion and minced garlic and stirring in 1 t. of cumin while it's cooking.

"One cannot think well, love well, sleep well, if one has not dined well."
– Virginia Woolf

*Luna Moth – isn't it beautiful? Don't worry, we didn't cook it.*

## Catsup Chicken

This is a dish I make all the time at home. It's messy and everyone raves about it. I've even made it for parties.

*Serves: 4*

*Ingredients:*
8 chicken legs (or any other part of the chicken you like)
olive oil
2 c. catsup (that's right, cups)
3-5 T. soy sauce
1 T. sugar
½ t. fresh or 1 t. of powdered ginger
1 or 2 stems scallions, cut thinly
red wine
paper napkins

*Preparation:*
1. Brown the chicken legs in 1 T. olive oil in a skillet.
2. Add 1 c. of catsup, 3 T. of soy sauce, 1 T. of sugar and the ginger. Add a big splash of red wine.
3. Mix everything to combine and bring it to a simmer.
4. Let the chicken simmer, half covered, until the meat is almost falling off the bones and the sauce has reduced to a sticky coating. Add more olive oil, catsup, soy sauce or red wine along the way to keep the pan from burning, according to your taste.
5. Sprinkle with sliced scallions.
6. Serve with napkins and forks.

"Hunger: One of the few cravings that cannot be appeased with another solution." – Irwin Van Grove

## Onion Rings

I love onion rings because they're such a clever way to get a child to eat an onion.

*Serves: 4*

*Ingredients:*
1 large yellow or Vidalia onion
½ c. white flour
½ t. baking soda
1 egg
2/3 c. milk
olive oil
salt & pepper
catsup

*Preparation:*
1. Slice the onion and separate the slices into rings.
2. Mix together the flour, baking soda and ½ t. each of salt & pepper.
3. Beat together the egg and the milk and add them to the dry ingredients, beating it all together well with a fork.
4. Heat 3 T. of olive oil to hot but not smoking.
5. Dip the onion rings one by one into the batter, then drop them into the frying pan.
6. Turn each ring after about 2 minutes, and when it's golden brown on both sides, remove it and drain it on paper towels.
7. You may need to add more oil as you go.
8. Serve with salt & pepper and catsup.

"I will not move my army without onions!" – Ulysses S. Grant

## String Cheese Logs

What's better than melted cheese inside a fresh biscuit?

*Serves: 6-8*

*Ingredients:*
1 tube refrigerated biscuits dough
1 package string cheese – 8-10 sticks
mild yellow mustard
aluminum foil

*Preparation:*
1. Wrap a piece of biscuit dough around a stick of string cheese.
2. Butter a double thick piece of aluminum foil and wrap the dough/cheese "log" in the foil.
3. Place the wrapped "log" on medium coals or on the hot part of the grill for about 10 minutes, turning often.
4. Serve with yellow mustard for dipping.

*Variations:*
- Wrap a slice of ham around the cheese before wrapping the biscuit dough around it.
- Try this with swiss cheese rolled into a stick.
- Use crescent rolls instead of biscuits.
- Spread mustard on the inside of the dough.
- Use spicy mustard for the grownups.

"A touch of these mustards brings out the flavor of Gruyère cheese, seasons a salad, gives a lift to white sauces, and gives style to a ragout. The hors d'oeuvre is the first dish to feel their good effect, which only ceases with the dessert."
– Paul Reboux

## Scooby Snacks

Yummy little nibbles that will make you popular with children.

*Feeds: 4*

*Ingredients:*
1 package pre-cooked breakfast sausages
8 strips bacon, cut into thirds
brown sugar
orange juice or apple cider
toothpicks

*Preparation:*
1. Cut each sausage in half, wrap it with a piece of bacon (1/3 of a strip) and secure it with a toothpick.
2. Dip each sausage/bacon/toothpick in juice and sprinkle it with brown sugar.
3. Cook the yummy little bundles on foil on the grill.
4. Bon appétit!

"What? Sunday morning in an English family and no sausages? God bless my soul, what's the world coming to, eh?" – Dorothy Sayers

## Christmas in July

My aunt and uncle bring a store-bought version of this sweet, curried cream cheese spread every Christmas. It is to-die-for delicious, and here's my homemade version, because I can't wait for Christmas.

*Serves: 4*

*Ingredients:*
1 8 oz. package cream cheese, softened (you can use reduced fat)
1 T. curry powder
5 T. mango chutney
1 T. sour cream or milk

*Preparation:*
1. Mash everything together until it's evenly blended.
2. Serve with crackers.
3. Try not to eat the whole thing.

*Variation:*
- The version my aunt and uncle bring actually has walnuts in it, so go ahead and add a small handful if you like nuts.

"Preach not to others what they should eat, but eat as becomes you, and be silent." – Epictetus

**More Starters**

Here are some starters that don't really need recipes …

1. Steamed or grilled clams with melted butter
2. Grilled shrimp – see recipe in the Main Dish section
3. Chilled shrimp with cocktail sauce – once when we camped in Maine a local friend brought over chilled shrimp and cocktail sauce! What a glamorous treat! I wouldn't bring this from home, though; I would buy it locally, cooked and chilled, and eat it that day.
4. Raw oysters from a jar wrapped in bacon and grilled
5. Chunks of sausage wrapped in bacon and grilled
6. Bruschetta – top a piece of toast with chopped tomatoes mixed with olive oil, minced garlic (or garlic powder) and salt & pepper
7. Mini pizzas on mini pita bread
8. Quesadillas – see the recipe in the Main Dish section.
9. Pretzels made with refrigerated biscuit dough, cooked over the fire on sticks, sprinkled with sea salt and served with mustard.
10. Smoked salmon and cream cheese (or smoked salmon flavored cream cheese) on tortillas – rolled up and sliced into pinwheels
11. Ham roll-ups – with cream cheese inside, rolled up and sliced
12. Salami roll-ups - with cream cheese and mustard
13. Mozzarella, tomato and basil salad, drizzled with oil & vinegar
14. Hardboiled eggs cut lengthways into quarters and sprinkled with salt & paprika
15. Paté or liverwurst with butter and rye bread
16. Smoked oysters and crackers
17. Tuna salad on crackers – we use olive oil and lemon juice instead of mayo
18. Goat cheese, pears and crackers
19. String cheese
20. Crudité with ranch, blue cheese or onion dip
21. Celery sticks stuffed with peanut butter or cream cheese; add raisins for "ants on a log"
22. "New" pickles (the crunchy ones)
23. Chips and salsa or guacamole
24. Chips and hummus or baba ghanoush
25. Potato chips, pretzels, cheese puffs, Cheetos or my personal favorite, Doritos

"Hors D'oeuvre: A ham sandwich cut into forty pieces" – Jack Benny

# SNACKS

### Howard da Silva's famous Beef Jerky (make at home)

This is my father's recipe for beef jerky, made somewhat famous in an article in the L.A. Times in 1976 (Johna Blinn, *Cooking Needs a Sense of Humor*, 6/23/76). When my Dad made this it drove my Mom crazy because he left the oven on all night to dry out the jerky.

*Serves: 8*

*Ingredients:*
3 lbs. lean London Broil
¾ c. soy sauce
¼ c. Worcestershire sauce
1 T. honey
2 T. catsup or barbecue sauce
¼ t. garlic powder
salt & pepper to taste

*Preparation:*
1. Slice the meat diagonally across the grain with a very sharp knife or meat cleaver into strips ¼" thick x 4" long. Set the meat aside.
2. Combine the remaining ingredients in a mixing bowl. Mix well.
3. Pour the marinade over the beef strips in a shallow glass dish. Marinate 30 minutes, turning the meat several times.
4. Arrange the beef on cake racks placed on cookie sheets lined with aluminum foil.
5. Place the racks in a preheated 180 degree F. oven for 12 hours or overnight.
6. The next morning, remove the jerky from the racks. Cool to room temperature before storing in airtight jars.

"I am a great eater of beef, and I believe that does harm to my wit." – William Shakespeare

## Popcorn

You can do it this way, or you can just buy Jiffy Pop. But I like the way this tastes better.

*Serves: 1*

*Ingredients:*
1 t. popcorn
1 t. olive oil
butter
aluminum foil

*Preparation:*
1. Make a large square of double-thick foil.
2. Put the oil and popcorn in the middle of the square.
3. Fold the foil over to make a pouch, and seal the edges. <u>Make sure you leave enough room for the popcorn to pop!</u>
4. Tie the pouch to a long stick and hold it over the fire.
5. Shake it until all the corn has popped.
6. Serve with salt and melted butter.

*TIP:*
- You can also do this in a Dutch Oven. Oil the bottom well and put in about ¼ of a cup of popcorn. Cook it on the coals until all the corn has popped.

"The laziest man I ever met put popcorn in his pancakes so they would turn over by themselves." – W. C. Fields

## Granola Bars (Make at Camp)

The kids like this more than they like real granola bars.

*Serves: 2*

*Ingredients:*
6 packets instant oatmeal, apple cinnamon flavor
¾ stick of butter

*Preparation:*
1. Melt ¾ of a stick of butter in a skillet over low heat.
2. Add the instant oatmeal and stir it around until it is well mixed and the chunks of sugar and flavoring melt.
3. Pat down the oatmeal into a solid cake.
4. After the oatmeal has cooked for about 2 minutes, flip it over and cook it on the other side. Cook on the other side for 2 or 3 more minutes.
5. Slide the oatmeal cake onto a plate, cut it into 4 quarters and let it harden, or eat it while it's still warm and soft.

"Remember the days when you let your child have some chocolate if he finished his cereal? Now, chocolate is one of the cereals." – Robert Orben

## Granola Bars (Make at Home)

Chocolate chips for that natural burst of energy.

*Serves: 6 (2 bars each)*

*Ingredients:*
4 c. granola
½ c. brown sugar
1 stick butter, melted
½ c. peanut butter
½ c. chocolate chips
½ c. chopped macadamia nuts

*Preparation:*
1. Mix together the sugar, butter and peanut butter with a fork until well blended.
2. Add the granola, chocolate chips and nuts.
3. Press the mixture down into a buttered pan and bake at 300 degrees for 20 minutes.
4. Cut into 12 bars and cool.

"Do you know what breakfast cereal is made of? It's made of all those little curly wooden shavings you find in pencil sharpeners!" – Roald Dahl, *Charlie and the Chocolate Factory*

## Gorp

It's the M&Ms that make it so healthy.

*Serves: 8*

*Ingredients:*
2 c. raisins, Craisins, dried pineapple, banana chips or dried apricots
2 c. peanuts, almonds or macadamia nuts
1 c. dark chocolate chips, peanut butter chips or M&Ms

*Preparation:*
1. Mix everything together.
2. Divide the gorp into 8 little Ziploc bags.
3. Serve to 8 hungry, little campers.

"In the cookie of life, friends are chocolate chips." – Salman Rushdie

## Potato Chips

Possibly my favorite thing ever.

*Serves: 2-4*

*Ingredients:*
2 large potatoes, sliced thinly
olive oil
salt & pepper

*Preparation:*
1. Bring a large pot of water to boil.
2. Meanwhile, take a long piece of foil and fold in half to make it double-thick. With a sharp knife, poke 20-30 small holes in it.
3. Boil the potato slices for about 1 minute.
4. Drain the potatoes.
5. Oil the foil, place it on the grill over medium-hot coals and cover it with a layer of potato slices.
6. Brush oil on the potato slices and sprinkle them with salt & pepper.
7. Cook for about 5 minutes, then turn the potatoes over.
8. Salt and pepper the other side and cook for another 5 minutes, until browned.
9. Put the cooked chips on paper towels to soak up any oil.
10. Cook the rest of the chips in batches.
11. Add additional salt and pepper to taste.

"Potato chips, potato chips, I love potato chips. Potato chips, potato chips, eat 'em up, wow." – Radio Jingle

## Fruit Dip

The kids think this is fancy.

*Serves: 4*

*Ingredients:*
1 8 oz. container whipped cream cheese
1 T. sugar, or more to taste
1 T. orange juice
1 T. sour cream

*Preparation:*
1. Mix all of the ingredients together with a fork until well blended.
2. Serve with strawberries, pineapple chunks on toothpicks, apple and orange slices or any other kind of fruit you like.

"Love is a fruit in season at all times, and within reach of every hand."
– Mother Teresa

# MAIN DISHES

Spider Dogs

MAGGIE DA SILVA

# SANDWICHES

**Grilled Club**

You can make this in a skillet, sandwich iron or just wrapped in a piece of foil.

*Serves: 1*

*Ingredients:*
2 slices bread
2 strips bacon
2 slices turkey
2 slices cheese such as Provolone or Swiss
butter
mustard and mayonnaise

*Preparation:*
1. Butter both sides of both slices of bread.
2. Place one slice of bread in a skillet, butter-side down, and cover with one slice of cheese.
3. Lay the turkey on top of the cheese.
4. Top with the 2nd slice of buttered bread.
5. When browned on the bottom, flip the sandwich. Cover the skillet and let the sandwich brown and the cheese melt.
6. Serve with mustard and mayo - the kids can put a little of each on their plates and dip their sandwiches in them.

*Variations:*
- Add tomato slices and/or pickles.
- Spread pesto on one or both slices of bread.
- Serve with chips.

"Call me All-American, but I love ham and cheese sandwiches. And not just any old ham and cheese sandwich... My mother's is the best. I've tried many times to make these sandwiches on my own, but it's never the same." – Andy Roddick

## Grilled Cheese and Curry

An easy way to make a grilled cheese sandwich even more thrilling.

*Serves: 1*

*Ingredients:*
2 slices bread
2 slices cheese – I like cheddar with this
curry powder
butter
salt & pepper

*Preparation:*
1. Melt 1 T. of butter in a skillet, and add one slice of bread.
2. Lay both slices of cheese on the bread.
3. Sprinkle the cheese with 1 t. curry powder.
4. Butter 2nd slice of bread, and lay it butter-side down on the sandwich in the skillet.
5. When browned on the bottom, flip the sandwich. Cover the skillet and let the sandwich brown and the cheese melt.

*Variation:*
- Try with sliced tomatoes, olives or thinly sliced scallions.

"I went into a French restaurant and asked the waiter, 'Have you got frog's legs?' He said, 'Yes,' so I said, 'Well hop into the kitchen and get me a cheese sandwich.'" – Tommy Cooper

## Grilled Peanut Butter

This is probably what Elvis ate when he went camping. We usually make these in a skillet, but they're also yummy in a sandwich iron.

*Serves: 1*

*Ingredients:*
2 T. peanut butter
2 slices bread
1 T. butter

Preparation:
1. Make a peanut butter sandwich.
2. Fry the sandwich in butter.
3. Cool and eat the sandwich.

*Variation:*
- Add a sliced banana, a piece of chocolate, a strip of cooked bacon or a marshmallow to your sandwich. Or add all four!

"After a hard day of basic training, you could eat a rattlesnake." – Elvis Presley

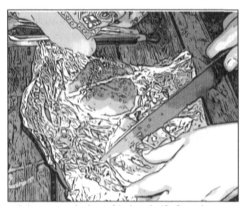
*Bring a good, sharp kitchen knife from home.*

## Pizza Bagel

Excellent for cheering up grumpy campers.

*Serves: 1*

*Ingredients:*
1 bagel
2 slices Mozzarella or Provolone cheese
4 T. spaghetti sauce
4 oz. pepperoni, sausage or even hamburger
aluminum foil

*Preparation:*
1. Make a cooking sheet out of a double thickness of foil.
2. Place the bagel halves on the foil.
3. Spread spaghetti sauce on both bagel halves, then add the cheese and pepperoni on top.
4. Place the foil with the pizza on the grill and cook until the cheese has melted and the bagel is lightly browned.
5. Bon appétit!

*Variations:*
- Use pita bread, tortillas or biscuits instead of bagels. Pitas and tortillas can be placed directly on the grill as they are bigger and won't fall through
- Add sautéed spinach or mushrooms to the pizza.
- Use a pie iron with slices of bread buttered on both sides.
- Serve with some warmed-up marinara sauce for dipping.
- Try a sprinkle of Parmesan cheese on top.

"There's a pizza place near where I live that sells only slices. In the back you can see a guy tossing a triangle in the air." – Stephen Wright

## Meatball Wedges

That's what we call them where I come from. Otherwise known as Heroes, Grinders and Subs.

*Serves: 4*

*Ingredients:*
16 frozen meatballs – I make my own but you can buy frozen ones at the supermarket. Even IKEA has edible meatballs.
1 jar marinara sauce
4 hamburger rolls – you can use hero rolls, but I never remember to buy them.
½ lb. Mozzarella cheese
grated Parmesan cheese
salt & pepper

*Preparation:*
1. Empty the jar of marinara into a skillet and bring to a simmer.
2. Add the meatballs and return to a simmer.
3. Place two slices of Mozzarella cheese on each roll and grill the roll until the cheese melts.
4. When the meatballs are heated through, spoon 4 meatballs with plenty of sauce onto each roll. Sprinkle with Parmesan cheese.
5. Serve with salt & pepper and Parmesan cheese.

*Variations:*
- Substitute sausages for meatballs. Grill whole Italian sausages and put them whole or sliced on the buns.
- Substitute BBQ sauce for marinara.

"Miracles are like meatballs, because nobody can exactly agree on what they are made of, where they come from, or how often they should appear."
– Lemony Snicket

## Cheesesteaks

Real Philly Cheesesteaks are made with Cheese Whiz! But I like regular American cheese on mine, sue me.

*Serves: 4*

*Ingredients:*
1 lb. flank steak
1 small, yellow onion, sliced medium-thin
8 slices American cheese
4 hot dog rolls
olive oil or butter
salt & pepper, catsup and A1 sauce

*Preparation:*
1. Slice the onion and cook it in a skillet in 1 T. oil or butter until the onions are soft and a little brown. Remove the onions from the skillet.
2. Slice the steak into thin strips and cook them in the skillet with a little extra oil.
3. While the steak is cooking, put 2 slices of cheese on each hot dog roll and grill the rolls until the cheese has melted.
4. Divide the steak and onions among the 4 hot dog rolls.
5. Serve with salt & pepper, catsup and A1 sauce. Bon appétit!

*Variations:*
- Serve with sautéed red & green peppers or sautéed mushrooms.
- Try Cheese Whiz! That's how they do it in Philly.
- You can also cook the meat and onions in aluminum foil on the grill.

"Too few people understand a really good sandwich." – James Beard

## Grilled Chicken Sandwiches

A great lunch when you didn't use up all your chicken the night before.

*Serves: 4*

*Ingredients:*
1 lb. chicken cutlets or boneless chicken breasts sliced thin
4 hamburger rolls
olive oil
mayonnaise
shredded lettuce and tomato slices, for topping
salt & pepper and hot sauce

*Preparation:*
1. Brush the chicken with olive oil and grill it until tender.
2. Meanwhile, warm up the hamburger buns on the grill.
3. Divide the chicken among the 4 rolls.
4. Slather both sides of the bun with mayonnaise.
5. Top with lettuce and tomato.
6. Serve with salt & pepper and hot sauce.

*Variations:*
- Add cheese to the buns when you're warming them up.
- Add some pesto to the mayonnaise.
- Marinate the chicken in Teriyaki sauce in a Ziploc bag for a few hours before grilling.

"Enjoy every sandwich." – Warren Zevon

## Cheeseburgers

I know you know how to make a cheeseburger. But just in case.

*Serves: 4*

*Ingredients:*
1 lb. ground beef, which is no more than 80% lean
4 hamburger rolls
4 slices of American cheese
olive oil
shredded lettuce, sliced tomato and sliced red onions, for topping
salt & pepper, hot sauce, catsup, mayonnaise and A1 sauce

*Preparation:*
1. In a bowl, gently mix the hamburger with 1 t. of. salt and ½ t. of pepper. Don't mush the burger around, just mix it once.
2. Divide the burger into 4 parts and gently make 4 patties. Don't make them too flat.
3. Put a little oil on each side of each patty and place them on the hot grill.
4. Depending on the thickness of the burgers, grill them about 3 minutes each side. Don't press down on the patty while it's grilling – that squeezes the juices out into the fire and makes the burgers dry.
5. Take the burgers off the grill and let them sit for a minute.
6. Lay the cheese on the buns and toast them until the cheese melts.
7. Add burgers to buns.
8. Top with lettuce, tomato and red onions.
9. Serve with salt & pepper, hot sauce, catsup, mayonnaise and A1 sauce.

*Variations:*
- Try blue cheese – that's my favorite.
- Let the kids cook their burgers in an onion in the fire - hollow out half an onion and squish a hamburger patty inside it. Wrap it in foil and place it in the coals for about 20 minutes.
- Wrap a handful of burger around a stick and cover the burger with foil. Cook it over the fire like a hot dog. (Kids enjoy this but it's kind of messy.)

"Anybody who doesn't think that the best hamburger place in the world is in his home town is a sissy." – Calvin Trillin

# PIE IRON COMBOS

**17 Pie Iron Sandwich Combinations**

It doesn't take a rocket scientist to use a pie iron: Heat it in the fire, open it up and add a pat of butter to each side. Put a slice of bread on each side, then put your fillings in between and shut the iron (and latch it if it has one). Trim any excess bread off the sides. Cook it in the coals for about 5 minutes.

Here are some suggested combinations:

1. Pizza: bread, marinara sauce, pepperoni or sausage and Mozzarella cheese (grease the pie iron with olive oil).
2. Ham and Cheese: try blue cheese.
3. Bacon, Tomato and Cheese (and every variation therein): add jalapenos for the grownups. Try with sundried tomatoes, or spicy mustard. Try with cream cheese or goat cheese.
4. Tuna Melt. 'Nuff said.
5. Pastrami and Swiss: try with mustard and sauerkraut.
6. Bacon Cheeseburger: use a hamburger bun in the pie iron instead of bread.
7. Sloppy Joe: use cooked ground beef and marinara sauce, and use a hamburger bun instead of bread.
8. Turkey and Cranberry Sauce: add some leftover stuffing.
9. Chicken Breast and Swiss: dip in Russian dressing after it's cooked.
10. Monte Cristo (ham, turkey, cheese, French toast): sprinkle plain bread with sugar for that French toast flavor.
11. Chicken Parmesan: sliced chicken, pizza sauce and Mozzarella cheese.
12. Smoked Salmon (or leftover cooked salmon) and cream cheese: add some scallions, too.
13. Quesadilla: cheese, chicken and cilantro filling, and use soft, flour tortillas instead of bread.
14. Mozzarella, Pesto and Peppers (roasted red peppers in a jar: mmm.)
15. Spaghetti Sandwich: leftover noodles and sauce with Mozzarella and Parmesan cheeses.
16. Veggies and Cheese: sautéed zucchini and tomato with Mozzarella cheese. We also like Feta cheese with this, and sometimes pesto sauce.
17. Butter and cinnamon sugar: now don't you feel better?

*Variations:*
- Try refrigerated dough instead of bread – such as piecrust, biscuit dough or

crescent rolls.
- While the kids are making the sandwiches, warm up some soup on the stove to go with it. We like clam chowder.
- Have fun!

"He's a couple sandwiches short of a picnic." – Lance Bass

*Packing the coolers is an artform! Use frozen bottles of water to keep things cool.*

# FOIL PACKETS

**Classic Burger Foil Packet with Variations**

The classic foil packet has a burger patty in the middle, but there are infinite variations of this. I've included a few of our favorites at the bottom.

*Serves: 1*

*Ingredients:*
4-8 oz. ground beef – as large as you want your patty
¼ small, yellow onion, chopped
½ medium potato, chopped
1/8 red and a green pepper, chopped
1 slice American cheese
olive oil, butter or spray oil to grease the foil
salt & pepper, hot sauce, catsup and A1 sauce
aluminum foil

*Preparation:*
1. Tear off a rectangle of aluminum foil and fold it in half to make a double thick square.
2. Grease the foil with olive oil, butter or spray oil.
3. Make a burger patty and lay it on the foil. Top the burger with the onion, potato and peppers. Dribble a little olive oil on top of the veggies and add salt and pepper to taste.
4. Wrap up the foil packet so the contents are snugly wrapped, but not too tight. Bend the ends of the packet to make handles for picking it up.
5. Place the packet directly on medium coals or on the hot part of the grill.
6. Turn every 5 minutes or so. Cook about 20 minutes, or until everything is cooked through. (You can check it often, that's part of the fun.)
7. Open up the packet. Top the burger and veggies with a slice of American cheese. Close the packet and let the steam melt the cheese (or pop the packet back on the fire for a minute to melt the cheese).
8. Serve with salt & pepper, hot sauce, catsup and A1 sauce.

*Variations:*
- Instead of burger patties, make individual meatloaves – mix the ground beef with an egg and seasoned breadcrumbs and a squirt of catsup or A1 sauce, or both! Then fashion the meat into mini loaves.
- Instead of ground beef, substitute dark meat turkey burger, sliced Italian sausage or Kielbasa, cubed steak or stew meat or sliced, raw chicken breast.

- Add a strip of cooked bacon to any of the above variations.
- Instead of meat, substitute shrimp or fish (omitting cheese).
- Try teriyaki sauce on your meat, and try sesame oil on your veggies.
- You can use all different kinds of veggies with this, depending on the meat and what you have on hand. Mushrooms and spinach go well with most things. Chicken and turkey like celery and carrots. Et cetera!
- Try different seasonings. We usually bring just a few, like oregano, basil, paprika and the ever-popular garlic powder.
- Try putting a pool of catsup under your burger or meatloaf before you cook it.
- Use tater tots or frozen hash browns instead of fresh potatoes.
- Bring cookie cutters and make fun shapes out of your burgers or meat loaves (for the little kids).

*TIP:*
- You can prepare these packets at home in advance. Let each kid put their packet together in your nice, clean kitchen with their nice, clean hands. Then write their names with a Sharpie on the top of the closed packets and they are ready to grill as soon as you get to camp. This is good if you want to serve these on the first night. You can also freeze the packets, which is great if you're cooking for a big group and want to make them a few days in advance.

"He ate tiny cheeseburgers in tin foil." – *Wag the Dog*

# QUESADILLAS, BURRITOS AND TACOS

## Quesadillas

These are easy to make no matter what your set-up is, and kids love them.

*Serves: 4*

*Ingredients:*
8 soft, flour tortillas
1 lb. Mexican, Jack or Mozzarella cheese, shredded
olive oil
chopped tomatoes, salsa and avocado for topping

*Preparation:*
1. In a skillet, brown a tortilla on one side.
2. Flip the tortilla and cover half of it with cheese.
3. Fold the tortilla in half, cover the pan and cook the quesadilla until the cheese is melted.
4. Cut into triangles.
5. Serve with chopped tomatoes, salsa and sliced avocados for topping.

*Variation:*
- Before folding the tortilla, add chopped, cooked chicken or steak and chopped white onion, tomatoes or other veggies.

"Cheese has always been a food that both sophisticated and simple humans love." – M.F.K. Fisher, *How to Cook a Wolf*

## Burritos

You can make these at home if you want to, then just warm them up on the grill or in the coals (wrapped twice in foil). We usually make our burritos with spinach, but feel free to substitute something else.

*Serves: 4*

*Ingredients:*
1 lb. ground beef
1 package frozen spinach, thawed
1 lb. shredded Mexican, Jack or Mozzarella cheese, shredded
4 large, soft, flour tortillas
salt & pepper, hot sauce and salsa

*Preparation:*
1. In a skillet, brown the hamburger and drain off any fat. Season with salt & pepper.
2. Add the thawed spinach to the hamburger and bring to a simmer.
3. Warm up the tortillas on the grill or over the camp stove.
4. Spoon the meat and spinach mixture into the tortillas, add a handful of grated cheese and roll up.
5. Serve with salt & pepper, hot sauce and salsa

*Variations:*
- Add a scoop of leftover rice inside the burrito or on the side. Use white or brown rice, or use instant yellow "Spanish" rice.
- Add guacamole or sour cream inside or on top of the burrito.
- Try dark meat turkey burger instead of hamburger.
- Use sausage or stew meat instead of hamburger.
- Serve with some warmed-up kidney beans or refried beans.
- Use different veggies, like sautéed zucchini, red and green peppers, onions, etc.
- For a vegetarian version, omit the meat and add refried beans inside the burrito.

"I was eating burritos with this girl and she asked me to be her prom date. How could I say no? We went and had a great time." – Josh Hartnett

**Tacos**

We usually make steak tacos, but you can put any meat you like in these.

*Serves: 4*

*Ingredients:*
4 corn tortillas
1 lb. flank steak
1 small, white onion, chopped and divided in half
1 clove garlic, minced
½ t. cumin
olive oil
1 large tomato, chopped
1 c. of cilantro, well washed and chopped
1 lime, quartered
salt & pepper, hot sauce and salsa

*Preparation:*
1. Grill the flank steak until medium-well done. Season with salt & pepper and slice into thin strips.
2. Heat 1T. of oil in the skillet. Add the garlic, cumin and ½ of the chopped onion. Cook until the onion is soft, being careful to not burn the garlic.
3. Add the steak to the onions and heat through.
4. Meanwhile, warm up the tortillas on the grill or over the camp stove, and stack them to keep them warm.
5. Divide the meat and onions among the tortillas and top with chopped cilantro, raw onion and tomato. Add a squeeze of lime.
6. Serve with salt & pepper, hot sauce, salsa and extra limes to squeeze onto the tacos.
7. Disfrutan!

*Variations:*
- Substitute chicken for steak. Grill a chicken breast and when it's cool, shred it with your fingers.
- A lot of people like their tacos topped with shredded cheese, like Mexican, Jack or Mozzarella.
- Top with guacamole or salsa.

"Bread and butter, devoid of charm in the drawing-room, is ambrosia eating under a tree." – Elizabeth Russell

# PASTA

### Macaroni 'N' Cheese

Make sure to bring some foil pie tins with you – the kids use them all the time to put together dishes like this.

*Serves: 4*

*Ingredients:*
1 lb. elbow macaroni
1 lb. Cheddar cheese, shredded
¼ c. milk
butter – 1 T. per pie pan
Parmesan cheese, grated
seasoned breadcrumbs
salt & pepper and hot sauce
4 aluminum foil pie pans
aluminum foil

*Preparation:*
1. Bring a big pot of salted water to boil for the pasta.
2. Cook the macaroni to al dente and drain. (Don't overcook it as it's also going on the grill.)
3. Let the kids make their own mac 'n' cheese combos in individual pie pans, mixing up cooked macaroni, shredded cheddar and a little milk. Have them mix their ingredients well and sprinkle with breadcrumbs and Parmesan. Cover the mixture with dots of butter – about 1 T. total per pie tin.
4. Cover the pans with foil and cook on the grill, about 10 minutes until the cheese and butter are melted.
5. Stir the mac 'n' cheese again before serving it to mix up the cheese sauce.
6. Bon appétit!

*Variations:*
- Omit the breadcrumbs for a smoother consistency.
- Add ½ cup of cooked veggies to each pie plate. Try peas and carrots, canned corn, sautéed spinach, cooked frozen peas, edamame or fresh, chopped tomatoes.
- Use Mozzarella or American cheese instead of Cheddar.
- Used crumbled crackers, like Ritz, instead of breadcrumbs.
- Add ¼ c. cooked and drained ground beef or a couple of ounces of diced ham to each serving.

- Use boxes of instant mac 'n' cheese, such as Kraft brand. I like it, and it has that special orange color you can't find anywhere else except on Doritos.

*TIP:*
- This is another dish you can make at home if you want to. Cover with foil and mark each child's name with a sharpie. You can even slip each tin into a gallon-sized Ziploc bag and freeze it.

"Macaroni and cheese! We gotta make this!" – Steve (the stoned guy) on *Friends*

Site 42, somewhere in New Jersey

## Chicken Parmesan Fettuccini

This is a delicious, simple dish that covers all of the four food groups (well, basically). If your kids don't like marinara sauce you can just toss the noodles and chicken with a little olive oil and Parmesan.

*Serves: 4*

*Ingredients:*
2 boneless chicken breasts
1 jar marinara sauce
1 lb. fettuccini
olive oil
8 oz. Mozzarella cheese, shredded
salt & pepper and grated Parmesan cheese

*Preparation:*
1. Bring a big pot of salted water to boil for the pasta.
2. Meanwhile, brush the chicken breasts with olive oil and grill them until they're done but tender.
3. Cool the chicken and slice it or pull it apart with your fingers.
4. Cook the fettuccini to al dente and drain.
5. Warm the sauce in a skillet. Add the chicken and bring to a simmer.
6. Return the noodles to the noodle pot, add the sauce and chicken and mix.
7. Dish onto plates and top with a handful of shredded mozzarella.
8. Serve with salt & pepper and grated Parmesan cheese.

*Variations:*
- You can add the cheese to the pot and mix it in, but it makes it a lot harder to clean the pot!
- This makes a good foil dinner as well.
- Try adding some veggies to the noodles while they're cooking, like frozen peas and carrots or spinach.

"What is sauce for the goose may be sauce for the gander but is not necessarily sauce for the chicken, the duck, the turkey or the guinea hen."
– Alice B. Toklas

## Spaghetti with Meat Sauce

To mix or not to mix? If your kids have differing opinions about mixing in the sauce, serve them each a bowl of plain noodles with a dollop of sauce on the side. Then they can mix or not as they like.

*Serves:* 4

*Ingredients:*
¾ lb. lean hamburger
1 jar marinara sauce
½ small, yellow onion, chopped
1 clove garlic, minced
salt & pepper and grated Parmesan cheese

*Preparation:*
1. Bring a big pot of salted water to boil for the pasta.
2. Meanwhile, cook the onions and garlic in 1 T. of olive oil in your skillet, being careful to not burn the garlic.
3. Add the hamburger to the onions and garlic, working it with a wooden spoon to break up the clumps while it's cooking.
4. Add the noodles to the boiling water, cook until al dente and drain.
5. Add the marinara sauce to the hamburger and bring to a simmer.
6. Return the noodles to the big pot and toss with a little olive oil.
7. Dish the pasta onto plates and put a dollop of sauce towards the side of each plate.
8. Serve with grated Parmesan cheese and salt & pepper.

*Variations:*
- Add sliced mushrooms, chopped peppers or zucchini to the meat and onions.
- Serve with shredded Mozzarella cheese.
- Instead of real pasta, use canned spaghetti, like Chef Boyardee! I love this (don't judge!) but the kids think it's too gloppy. If you do use the canned spaghetti, make sure you serve it with Wonderbread and margarine. Mmm.

"Everything you see I owe to spaghetti." – Sophia Loren

MAGGIE DA SILVA

**Pasta Salad**

It wouldn't be a salad without cheese and sausage! This is very easy to prepare and the leftovers keep well.

*Serves: 4-6*

*Ingredients:*
1 lb. farfalle pasta (bowties), or any other shape you like
6 links cooked Italian sausage or Kielbasa, sliced
8 oz. firm Mozzarella cheese, cubed
1 small, red onion, chopped
1 tomato, chopped
¾ c. pitted Kalamata or black olives
olive oil
red wine vinegar
salt & pepper

*Preparation:*
1. Bring a big pot of salted water to boil for the pasta.
2. Add the noodles to the boiling water, cook until al dente and drain.
3. Cut the Mozzarella into small cubes.
4. Chop the onions and tomatoes.
5. Add the pasta, sausage, Mozzarella, onions, tomatoes and olives back to the big pot.
6. Dress with oil and vinegar and salt & pepper. Toss gently.
7. Serve with salt & pepper.

*Variations:*
- This is great with a few fresh basil leaves thrown in.
- Sundried tomatoes are nice instead of fresh tomatoes.
- Serve with Parmesan cheese to sprinkle on top.

"When the phone rang I was in the kitchen, boiling a potful of spaghetti and whistling along with an FM broadcast of the overture to Rossini's 'The Thieving Magpie,' which has to be the perfect music for cooking pasta."
– Haruki Murakami, *The Wind-Up Bird Chronicle*

## Tortellini Primavera

This recipe requires some chopping. You can chop all the veggies at home or you can just leave some of them out. But at the very least, wash all of your veggies at home, because it saves a lot of time and grit at the campsite.

*Serves: 4-6*

*Ingredients:*
3 10 oz. packages tortellini
1 medium, yellow onion, chopped
1 clove garlic, minced
¼ red and a green pepper, chopped
1 small zucchini, chopped
1 carrot, peeled and cut into matchsticks
1 c. of frozen spinach, defrosted
4 oz. chicken broth
a splash of white wine, if you have it
olive oil
salt & pepper, grated Parmesan cheese and shredded Mozzarella cheese

*Preparation:*
1. Bring a big pot of salted water to boil for the pasta.
2. Meanwhile, cook the onions and garlic in 1 T. of olive oil in your skillet, being careful to not burn the garlic.
3. Add the carrots, peppers and zucchini to skillet and sauté for 3 minutes.
4. Add the spinach and bring to a simmer. Season the veggies with salt and pepper.
5. Add chicken broth and splash of white wine to the veggies.
6. Simmer another 3 or 4 minutes, until the broth is reduced by half. Taste and adjust seasonings.
7. Add the tortellini to the boiling water, cook until al dente and drain.
8. Return the tortellini to the big pot, and add the veggies and sauce from the skillet.
9. Serve with salt & pepper, Mozzarella and Parmesan.

*Variations:*
- You can add the cheese to the pot but it makes it a lot harder to clean the pot!
- If you don't have wine or broth, chop a tomato into the skillet, and add a little more oil and a little water. Or just cook all the veggies in butter.

"No man is lonely while eating spaghetti." – Robert Morley

## Pasta with Pesto

Making pesto is easy (at home): Put a large handful of washed basil, a large handful of grated Parmesan and a small handful of raw walnuts in a blender with about ½ of a cup of olive oil. Blend until creamy. There, you're done. Now freeze it so you can bring it camping. Or just buy a container of pesto, it's usually with the hummus in the supermarket.

*Serves:* 4

*Ingredients:*
1 lb. Penne pasta, or any shape you like
¼ c. pesto sauce
salt & pepper and grated Parmesan cheese

*Preparation:*
1. Bring a big pot of salted water to boil for the pasta.
2. Add the pasta to the boiling water, cook until al dente and drain.
3. Return the pasta to the big pot and toss with the pesto sauce.
4. Serve with salt & pepper and grated Parmesan cheese.

*Variation:*
- Add some frozen peas or other veggies to the pasta water.

"Pesto is the quiche of the '80s." – Nora Ephron

## Linguini with Clam Sauce

A fabulous Day 4 or 5 dinner, and if we don't tell the kids this has clams in it, they gobble it up.

*Serves: 4*

*Ingredients:*
1 lb. Linguini
1 6 oz. jar minced clams with juice
¼ c. olive oil
4 oz. white wine
8 oz. chicken broth
1 small, yellow onion, chopped
1 clove garlic, minced
anchovy paste in a tube
salt & pepper and grated Parmesan cheese

*Preparation:*
1. Bring a big pot of salted water to boil for the pasta.
2. Add the pasta to the boiling water, cook until al dente and drain.
3. Sauté the onion and garlic in 1 T. of olive oil until soft.
4. Mix 1" of anchovy paste into the onion with a fork.
5. Add the broth, white wine and the juice from the clams.
6. Simmer about 20 minutes, then add the clams and bring back to a simmer.
7. Return the linguini to the big pot with the clam sauce and toss gently.
8. Serve with salt & pepper and grated Parmesan cheese.

"It is not a matter of indifference whether we like oysters or clams, snails or shrimp, if only we know how to unravel the existential significance of these foods." – Jean-Paul Sartre

# MEAT DISHES

**Steak**
We usually have steak the first night.

*Serves: 2*

*Ingredients:*
1 nice, fatty steak, about 16 oz. We usually eat chuck steak, but if we're feeling fancy we'll get a strip steak or a ribeye.
olive oil
salt & pepper

*Preparation:*
1. Rub the steak with olive oil and pepper both sides. (Save the salt for later.)
2. Let the steak warm up a bit while you build your fire.
3. When you have hot coals, lay the steak on the grill – you should hear a sizzle when you lay the steak down. If the fat catches on fire, move the steak to a slightly cooler spot.
4. Grill the steak 2-5 minutes on each side, depending on the thickness of steak. When the bottom of the steak turns color and you have sear marks on the bottom, turn it.
5. Don't be shy about checking your steak. It's better to undercook it than over cook it. Stick a knife in the middle and press back the meat to check it. We like ours red on the inside, but not blue.
6. Take your steak off, flip it just-cooked side up and let it rest for a couple of minutes so the juices distribute throughout.
7. Serve with salt & pepper. We don't generally put sauce on our steak, but if you have something you like, bring it along.

*Variations:*
- This is crying out for a baked potato, so wrap a couple in foil and stick them in the fire early on, or prebake a few at home and just warm them up in the fire.
- Serve with a pat of butter or a dollop of salsa on top.
- This is also nice with creamed spinach (frozen, boil in a bag).

"When I go out, I love steak and caviar." – Cameron Diaz

## Steak Salad

A delicious lunch on day 2 with your still-fresh lettuce and leftover steak. Wash your lettuce at home, dry it well and pack it in a Ziploc bag with a paper towel to absorb any moisture.

*Serves: 2*

*Ingredients:*
2 c. Romaine lettuce
1 perfectly cooked steak, still warm, about 16 oz.
olive oil & vinegar
salt & pepper

*Preparation:*
1. Tear lettuce into medium pieces and put into a salad bowl.
2. Dress the greens with oil and vinegar and salt & pepper. Put some on each plate.
3. Slice steak and divide between plates.
4. Salt and pepper steak.
5. Bon appétit!

*Variation:*
- We also like this with a wedge of Iceberg lettuce and blue cheese dressing.

"To make a good salad is to be a brilliant diplomatist – the problem is entirely the same in both cases. To know how much oil one must mix with one's vinegar." – Oscar Wilde

## Beef Kebabs

We cut up everything at home and pack it in separate Ziploc bags. Then the kids assemble the kebabs at the campsite. Remember to bring potholders because the metal skewers get hot.

*Serves: 4*

*Ingredients:*
2 lbs. sirloin tips, cut into bite-sized pieces
1 green pepper, cut into bite-sized pieces
1 red pepper, cut into bite-sized pieces
1 red onion, cut into bite-sized pieces
1 lb. cherry tomatoes
10 oz. whole mushrooms, halved
olive oil
lemons
salt & pepper, mild BBQ sauce, A1 sauce and catsup
metal (or wooden) skewers – at least 9" long

*Preparation:*
1. If you're using wooden skewers, soak them in water for a while so they don't burn on the grill.
2. Clean and cut up your veggies into bite-sized pieces. Cut the mushrooms in half.
3. Cut the meat into bite-sized pieces.
4. Let the kids create their own kebabs, alternating the ingredients on the skewers.
5. Pour some olive oil into a plate and let the kids roll their kebabs in the oil.
6. Place the kebabs on the grill and pepper them.
7. After a couple of minutes, flip the kebabs.
8. Remove the kebabs from grill and squeeze lemon on them.
9. Serve with salt & pepper, mild BBQ sauce, A1 sauce and catsup.

*Variations:*
- Substitute chicken or turkey breast for steak.
- Serve with baked potatoes from the fire.
- Mix some minced garlic into the oil before you dip the kebabs. (Bring a jar of that minced garlic you buy in the store.)
- Serve with pita bread and let each kid make a sandwich out of kebabs and pita. Try this with yogurt dressing – plain yogurt, a little garlic & lemon, salt to taste.
- Try some fruit on your kebabs, like pineapple, apple or peach.

- Add a few shrimp. They like to be basted in butter.
- Serve with rice.

"Beef is the soul of cooking." – Marie-Antoine Carême

*Remember to pack the rope!*

## Marinated Flank Steak

Flank steak likes to be marinated and the kids like teriyaki sauce.

*Serves: 2, or 4 dainty people*

*Ingredients:*
16 oz. flank steak
1 c. teriyaki sauce
3 cloves garlic, minced
¼ c. pineapple juice
5 T. brown sugar
1 T. soy sauce

*Preparation:*
1. Put everything except the steak into a large Ziploc bag and mix well.
2. Add the steak and marinate overnight, all day or at least for a couple of hours.
3. Grill 2-3 minutes on each side.
4. Slice the steak and serve with baked potatoes.

*Variations:*
- Try a different kind of juice, like apple or papaya.
- We also like jerk seasoning on our steak, but it's too spicy for kids.

"Give them great meals of beef and iron and steel, they will eat like wolves and fight like devils." – William Shakespeare, *King Henry V*

## Steak and Mushrooms

The kids like steak made this way, and sometimes I make hamburgers this way, too.

*Serves: 4*

*Ingredients:*
32 oz. London broil, sliced
10 oz. white mushrooms, sliced
1 small, yellow onion, chopped
½ c. white flour
2 c. beef broth
3 T. butter
salt & pepper

*Preparation:*
1. Melt butter in the bottom of a big pot or Dutch Oven.
2. Cook onions and mushrooms in the pot until the onions are soft.
3. Mix the flour and 1t. each of salt & pepper in a Ziploc bag.
4. In batches, dredge each strip of steak in flour, shake off the excess and braise in pot.
5. After all the meat is braised on both sides in butter, put it all back in the pot and add the beef broth.
6. Simmer for about 30 minutes, until the sauce thickens.
7. Serve over egg noodles or a baked potato.

"Nature alone is antique and the oldest art a mushroom." – Thomas Carlyle

## Steak on a stick

Did you forget your grill? Never fear.

*Serves: 2-4*

*Ingredients:*
16 oz. strip steak, sliced
olive oil
salt & pepper, BBQ sauce, catsup and A1 sauce
long, sturdy skewers or green, pointy sticks

*Preparation:*
1. Thread the steak slices onto the sticks.
2. Rub the steak with olive oil and pepper.
3. Roast over coals until done – Just a couple of minutes per side.
4. Serve with salt & pepper, BBQ sauce, catsup and A1 sauce

"I dined on what they called 'robber steak' – bits of bacon, onion, and beef, seasoned with red pepper, and strung on sticks and roasted over the fire, in the simple style of the London cat meat!" – Jonathan Harker in Bram Stoker's *Dracula*

## Lamb chops

Don't cook these wee chops too long.

*Serves: 4-6*

*Ingredients:*
8 lamb chops
2 cloves garlic
½ c. olive oil
salt & pepper
fresh rosemary

*Preparation:*
1. In a large Ziploc bag, mix together garlic and olive oil with 1 t. of pepper. Tear a big sprig of rosemary into a few pieces and mix that in.
2. Add the lamb chops to the marinade and zip it shut. Turn the chops bag over a few times while the fire is getting hot.
3. When the coals are hot, grill the lamb chops 2-4 minutes on each side.
4. Bon appétit!

*Variation:*
- Serve with baked potatoes or potato/veggie packets.

"If you throw a lamb chop in the oven, what's to keep it from getting done?"
– Joan Crawford in *The Women*

## Dutch Oven Pork Chops

This is a good one for the Dutch Oven as it doesn't require much checking and it always turns out fantastic.

*Serves: 4*

*Ingredients:*
4 pork chops
½ small, yellow onion, chopped
2 large potatoes, cubed
4 carrots, peeled and sliced
2 T. olive oil
2 c. beef broth
1 c. frozen peas
butter
salt & pepper, hot sauce and A1 sauce

*Preparation:*
1. Grill the pork chops on both sides to sear the meat, about 1 minute per side.
2. Grease the bottom of the Dutch Oven with olive oil.
3. Lay the potatoes on the bottom of the Dutch Oven.
4. Add the carrots and peas on top of the potatoes, and the onions on top of the carrots and peas.
5. On top of everything, lay the pork chops, and dot them liberally with butter.
6. Pour the beef broth over everything.
7. Cover and cook on hot coals for about 45 minutes. Check progress after about 30 minutes.

"There is poetry in a pork chop to a hungry man." – Philip Gibbs

## Pork Chop Foil Packet

Fun for the kids, and the thin cut chops cook quickly.

*Serves: 1*

*Ingredients:*
1 thin cut pork chop
1 small potato, sliced
1 carrot, peeled and sliced
olive oil
butter
salt & pepper, hot sauce and A1 sauce
aluminum foil

*Preparation:*
1. Tear off a rectangle of aluminum foil and fold it in half to make a double thick square.
2. Grease the foil with olive oil and butter.
3. Lay the pork chop on the foil and pepper the chop.
4. Add the potato and carrot, and dot with butter.
5. Wrap up the foil packet so the contents are snugly wrapped, but not too tight. Bend the ends of the packet to make handles for picking it up.
6. Place the packet directly on medium coals or on the hot part of the grill.
7. Turn every 5 minutes or so. Cook about 20 minutes, or until everything is cooked through. (You can check it often, that's part of the fun.)
8. Serve with salt & pepper, hot sauce and A1 sauce.

*Variation:*
- Wrap chop in strips of bacon.

"If you want a subject, look to pork!" – Charles Dickens, *Great Expectations*

## Meatballs and Spinach

A super-easy dish, and if your kids don't like spinach, this might convince them.

*Serves: 4*

*Ingredients:*
16-24 pre-cooked meatballs – I make my own but you can buy frozen ones at the supermarket.
1 package frozen spinach, thawed
2 c. beef or chicken broth
1 c. leftover cooked noodles
salt & pepper and grated Parmesan cheese

*Preparation:*
1. Bring the broth to a simmer in a big pot.
2. Add the meatballs, the spinach and the noodles. Return to a simmer.
3. Dish the meatballs and noodles into bowls and top with Parmesan cheese.
4. Serve with salt & pepper and more Parmesan cheese.

"Meat Meat! We are going to eat some meat; and what meat! Real game! Still no bread, though." – Ned Land in Jules Verne's *Twenty Thousand Leagues Under the Sea*

## Meatballs and Zucchini Foil Packets

For my zucchini-loving kid.

*Serves: 4*

*Ingredients:*
16-24 pre-cooked meatballs – I make my own but you can buy frozen ones at the supermarket.
2 zucchini, sliced
1 jar marinara sauce
Parmesan cheese, grated
crusty bread
aluminum foil

*Preparation:*
1. Tear off a rectangle of aluminum foil and fold it in half to make a double thick square.
2. Place 4-6 meatballs and a few slices of zucchini in the foil.
3. Cover everything with marinara, about ¼ c.
4. Wrap up the foil packet so the contents are snugly wrapped, but not too tight. Bend the ends of the packet to make handles for picking it up.
5. Place the packet directly on medium coals or on the hot part of the grill.
6. Turn the packet every 5 minutes or so. Cook it about 20 minutes, or until the zucchini is tender and the meatballs are hot. (You can check it often, that's part of the fun.)
7. Unfold the packets and sprinkle with Parmesan cheese.
8. Serve with extra warmed sauce.

*Variations:*
- You can just make this in a skillet also: Heat the sauce in a skillet, add the zucchini and simmer until soft, then add the meatballs and heat through.
- Serve with crusty bread.

"I am better off with vegetables at the bottom of my garden than with all the fairies of the Midsummer Night's Dream." – Dorothy L. Sayers

## Meatballs and Gravy

We all enjoy gravy in large quantities.

*Serves: 4*

*Ingredients:*
16-24 pre-cooked meatballs – I make my own but you can buy frozen ones at the supermarket
olive oil
2 T. butter
2 T. minced onion
2 c. beef broth
2 T. white flour

*Preparation:*
1. Lightly fry the meatballs in a little olive olive oil to warm them up. Set the meatballs aside and wipe out the skillet.
2. Melt the butter in the skillet and add the onion. Cook until soft.
3. Sprinkle the flour into the onions while stirring with a fork to mix evenly.
4. Stir in the broth little by little while whisking with the fork.
5. Simmer the gravy until it thickens and the flour is cooked, constantly whisking with a fork. Taste it to see if the flour is cooked – if it tastes like flour, it isn't cooked. If it has a browned, gravy flavor, it's cooked.
6. Divide the meatballs among your plates and cover with some of your delicious gravy.
7. Ooh la la.

*Variations:*
- Serve with crusty bread and/or cooked noodles.
- Go ahead, buy the IKEA meatballs and gravy mix. Just don't read the nutritional information. And don't forget the lingonberry sauce!

"A well made sauce will make even an elephant or a grandfather palatable."
– Grimod de la Reynière

## Hot Dog Hash

Hot dogs and eggs – a classic combination for college kids everywhere. We added the potatoes and veggies to class it up.

*Serves: 4*

*Ingredients:*
6 hot dogs
2 c. leftover cooked potatoes
½ c. frozen peas or leftover veggies
2 T. olive oil
5 eggs, lightly beaten
salt & pepper, hot sauce and catsup

*Preparation:*
1. Slice the hot dogs and simmer in 1 T. of olive oil in a skillet.
2. Add another T. of olive oil and add the potatoes and veggies and sauté until tender.
3. Add the scrambled eggs and let set. Mix gently and let set again.
4. Serve with salt & pepper, hot sauce and catsup.

"A hot dog at the ball park is better than steak at the Ritz." – Humphrey Bogart

## Pigs in Blankets

Kids love them, and so do I.

*Serves: 4-6*

*Ingredients:*
1 package hot dogs
1 tube refrigerated biscuit dough
American cheese
catsup and mustard
green, pointy sticks

*Preparation:*
1. Cook the hot dogs first in a pot of water or on sticks over the fire. Let cool.
2. Let kids put their hot dogs on sticks, wrap a slice of cheese around each dog and a piece of biscuit dough around the cheese.
3. Cook the dogs over the fire until the biscuit is golden brown and the cheese is melted.
4. Serve with mustard and catsup to dip into.

*Variations:*
- Top the dogs with chopped white onion, relish, or any other condiments you like.
- You can also make pigs in blankets with white bread in a pie iron. Split the dogs to do this.
- Try these wrapped in foil (this works better, actually, but it's not as much fun): oil foil and wrap it around hot dog/cheese/biscuit and place on hot coals or on grill. Flip a couple of times.
- Try with breakfast sausages.
- Try these with breadstick dough!

"Never eat more than you can lift." – Miss Piggy

## Barbecued Hot Dogs

Hot dogs again? Not so; these are fancy BBQ dogs.

*Serves: 4*

*Ingredients:*
4 hot dogs
4 hot dog buns
BBQ sauce

*Preparation:*
1. Put the hot dogs on the grill.
2. Brush them with BBQ sauce.
3. Cook them until done. Put them in buns with extra BBQ sauce. Eat up.

"Phrases and their actual meanings: 'My teacher has never liked me.' Expect a phone call before lunch from the teacher informing you that your child has been launching hot dogs by compressing them inside a small Thermos and then removing the lid quickly." – Erma Bombeck

## Hot Dog Tacos

Everything tastes better with American cheese. In a tortilla.

*Serves: 4*

*Ingredients:*
4 hot dogs
4 slices American cheese
4 corn tortillas

*Preparation:*
1. Cook the hot dogs over the open fire on sticks.
2. Warm the tortillas on the grill and stack them this keeps them warm.
3. Place 1 slice of American cheese inside a tortilla, followed by 1 hot dog.
4. Bon appétit!

"Ask not what you can do for your country, ask what's for lunch." – Orson Welles

## Spider Dogs

A classic. Never again will you roast a plain, old hot dog over the fire.

*Serves: 1*

*Ingredients:*
1 hot dog
catsup & mustard
a sharp knife
green, pointy sticks

*Preparation:*
1. Cut 4 slits on each end of the hot dog.
2. Put the hot dog on the stick in the center of the dog and cook it in the fire.
3. The slits will curl – those are the spider legs!
4. Eat on a with catsup & mustard.

"I have drunk, and seen the spider." – William Shakespeare

## Barbecued Ham

Another good recipe for later on in your trip. You can also substitute Spam, which never, ever goes bad.

*Serves: 4*

*Ingredients:*
1 lb. ham steak
mustard
brown sugar (or white sugar if you don't have brown)
olive oil

*Preparation:*
1. Mix ¼ c. of olive oil, 3 T. of sugar and 1 T. of mustard.
2. Brush the ham steak with sauce on both sides and grill over medium coals. Keep basting with the sauce and grill it until it's heated through and seared on both sides, not more than 5 minutes total, because the ham is pre-cooked.
3. Cut the ham into 4 pieces and serve with biscuits.

*Variation:*
- Serve with pineapple slices that have been grilled with a little brown sugar on top.

"Carve a ham as if you were shaving the face of a friend." – Henri Charpentier, cook to J.D. Rockefeller

## Ham au Gratin

Really yummy.

*Serves: 2-4*

*Ingredients:*
1 lb. ham steak
2 large potatoes, diced
1 small, yellow onion, minced
8 oz. Mozzarella cheese, shredded
1 c. milk
1 T. white flour
seasoned breadcrumbs
butter
salt & pepper

*Preparation:*
1. Cut the ham into bite-sized pieces.
2. Melt 3 T. of butter in a skillet and sauté the onion until it's soft.
3. Slowly sprinkle in the 1 T. of flour while whisking with a fork.
4. Add the milk slowly, whisking constantly with the fork, to make a white sauce.
5. Mix in the ham and potatoes until everything is evenly coated.
6. Sprinkle the mixture with cheese and breadcrumbs.
7. Cover and cook over the grill until the potatoes are tender, about 20 minutes.
8. Bon appétit!

*Variations:*
- Canadian bacon is a good substitute for ham.
- Add frozen green peas with the ham and potatoes.

"Pray for peace and grace and spiritual food, for wisdom and guidance, for all these are good, but don't forget the potatoes." – John Tyler Pettee

# STEWS

**Potatoes & Corn**

An easy and delicious way to include another veggie.

*Serves: 4*

*Ingredients:*
8 strips bacon
1 small, yellow onion, chopped
4 large potatoes, chopped
1 can corn or 2 ears of fresh corn
olive oil
salt & pepper

*Preparation:*
1. Cook the bacon in the bottom of a large pot and set aside. Wipe out about half of the bacon fat.
2. Chop the potatoes and fry them with onions in the bacon fat left in the pot. Add a little olive oil if needed. Cook until tender but not crispy.
3. Add the corn with half its juice from can, or add fresh ears of corn broken in half (4 pieces) and ½ c. of water.
4. Simmer about 5 minutes. Season with salt & pepper.

"The potato, like man, was not meant to dwell alone." – Shila Hibben

## Glop

There are infinite versions of camp stew made with leftovers. Here's one of ours.

*Serves: 4*

*Ingredients:*
3 or 4 links Italian sausage or Kielbasa
2 or 3 leftover cooked hamburgers
1 small, yellow onion, chopped
2 carrots, peeled and chopped
1/2 green and a red pepper, chopped
2 c. beef broth
2 c. leftover cooked noodles
olive oil
1 bay leaf
salt & pepper

*Preparation:*
1. Fry the sausages in the bottom of the pot in a little oil. Cool and slice the sausages.
2. Add 2 T. of olive oil to the pot and sauté the onions and the rest of the veggies with the bay leaf for about 5 minutes.
3. Add the noodles and sliced sausages and break up the leftover hamburgers into chunks in the pot.
4. Add the broth, mix gently and simmer for about 5 minutes.
5. Bon appétit!

*Variation:*
• Good with leftover cooked steak, too.

"If you never try a new thing, how can you tell what it's like? It's men such as you that hamper the world's progress. Think of the man who first tried German sausage!" – Jerome K. Jerome, *Three Men in a Boat*

## Sausages and Beans

We use edamame (soy beans) with this because our kids like them.

*Serves: 4*

*Ingredients:*
4 links Italian sausage or Kielbasa, sliced
1 small package frozen, shelled edamame, about 10 ounces
3 leftover cooked potatoes, chopped
olive oil
salt & pepper, hot sauce and catsup

*Preparation:*
1. Heat 2 T. of oil in a pot.
2. Fry the sausages in oil until they are cooked but not crispy.
3. Add the beans and the potatoes and cook about 3 minutes. Add a little water or broth if you need to.
4. Serve with salt & pepper, catsup and hot sauce.

*Variation:*
- Add a few strips of bacon. Cook the bacon in the pot, set it aside and wipe out about half the bacon fat. Proceed with frying the sausages, then add the bacon back in with the potatoes.

"Some people are fat, some people are lean. But I want you to show me the person who doesn't like butterbeans. Yay!" – B-52's, Butterbean

## Sausages and Cabbage

We make most of our stews with beef broth instead of tomatoes because we like it better.

*Serves: 4*

*Ingredients:*
4-6 links Italian sausage or Kielbasa, sliced
1 small, yellow onion, chopped
1 medium head cabbage, cut into eighths
3 potatoes, chopped
3 carrots, peeled and sliced
olive oil
2 c. beef broth
salt & pepper and mustard! Mustard is a must-have for this dish.
bay leaves

*Preparation:*
1. Heat 2 T. of oil in a pot.
2. Fry the sausages, onions and bay leaf in the oil until the sausages are cooked but not crispy.
3. Add the potatoes and cook about 5 minutes.
4. Add the carrots, cabbage and beef broth and simmer another 5 minutes or so, until cabbage is tender but still bright green.
5. Season with salt & pepper and dish out into bowls.
6. Serve with plenty of mustard.

*Variation:*
- You can add corn on the cob to this, broken into halves.

"Cabbage: A vegetable about as large and wise as a man's head." – Ambrose Bierce

## Sausages and Rice

Hearty and flavorful.

*Serves: 4*

*Ingredients:*
4-6 links Italian sausage or Kielbasa
1 c. rice
½ small, yellow onion, chopped
¼ green and a red pepper, chopped
2 stalks celery, chopped
2 c. beef broth
2 T. olive oil
about 10 green olives, sliced
2 t. turmeric – this makes the rice nice and yellow.
salt & pepper and hot sauce

*Preparation:*
1. Slice the sausages and cook them in the oil in a pot with the onion, pepper and celery.
2. Add the rice, olives and turmeric and stir well.
3. Add the broth and bring it to a simmer.
4. Cover the pot and simmer until the rice is tender.
5. Serve with salt & pepper and hot sauce.

*TIP:*
- Don't get turmeric on your clothes. It never comes out.

"Rice is the best, the most nutritive and unquestionably the most widespread staple in the world." – Escoffier

## Fried Rice-A-Roni

If you like Rice-A-Roni (and who doesn't) at home when you're all clean and comfortable, think of how much you'll love it when you're all cold and grimy.

*Serves: 4*

*Ingredients:*
1 box Rice-A-Roni, may I suggest one of their many chicken flavors
1 lb. cooked chicken breast, cubed
1 or 2 links pre-cooked sausage, sliced
1 c. frozen peas
2 eggs, lightly beaten
hot sauce

*Preparation:*
1. Prepare the Rice-A-Roni according to the directions in a pot. When it's time to stir in the water and the seasoning packet, stir in the chicken as well.
2. Cook the rice and chicken for 10 minutes, then add the sausage and peas.
3. Cook the mixture for 4 more minutes, then add the eggs.
4. Let the eggs set for about 2 minutes, then mix them gently into the rice. Let the eggs cook another 2 minutes, then mix them again. Remove the pot from the heat and cover it. Let it stand 5 minutes.
5. Serve with hot sauce. Rice-A-Roni needs no additional salt.

*Variations:*
- Try this with broccoli florets.
- Try this with cooked hamburger or meatballs instead of chicken and sausage.
- You can also make this recipe with plain, white rice and season it with soy sauce and a little sugar.

"The San Francisco Treat!" – Rice-A-Roni slogan

## Chicken Stew

Most people make chicken stew with tomatoes, but we make it with chicken broth and thicken it with flour.

*Serves: 4*

*Ingredients:*
8 strips bacon
1 lb. boneless chicken breast, cut into bite-sized pieces
1 small, yellow onion, chopped
2 potatoes, chopped
4 carrots, peeled and sliced
1 T. white flour
2 c. chicken broth
1 bay leaf
salt & pepper

*Preparation:*
1. Fry the bacon in the bottom of a big pot and set the bacon aside. Wipe out some of the bacon fat.
2. Cook the chicken in the bacon fat for about 5 minutes, stirring. Set the chicken aside.
3. Add the onions, potatoes, carrots and bay leaf to the pot, with a little olive oil if needed.
4. Sprinkle the flour into the pot and stir.
5. Add the broth and simmer about 10 minutes, until the potatoes are cooked and the sauce is thickened.
6. Add back the chicken and bacon and bring back to a simmer.
7. Serve with fresh biscuits.

*Variations:*
- Add a splash of white wine to this if you have some around.

"From time immemorial, soups and broths have been the worldwide medium for utilizing what we call the kitchen byproducts or as the French call them, the 'dessertes de la table' (leftovers), or 'les parties interieures de la bete', such as head, tail, lights, liver, knuckles and feet." – Louis P. DeGouy, *The Soup Book*

## Burger 'N' Beans

This combination of bacon, baked beans and brown sugar can't be beat.

*Serves: 4*

*Ingredients:*
1 lb. lean hamburger
6 strips bacon
1 can baked beans – I like Bush's Boston style.
1 small, yellow onion, chopped
2 potatoes, diced
1 T. brown sugar
yellow mustard
salt & pepper

*Preparation:*
1. Cook the bacon in a pot and set aside the bacon.
2. In the bacon fat, fry the onions, hamburger and potatoes until the hamburger is cooked.
3. Add the baked beans, a squirt of yellow mustard and the brown sugar.
4. Stir and cook until the potatoes are done, about 5 minutes.
5. Chop the bacon and sprinkle on top.
6. Serve with fresh biscuits.

"And this is good old Boston, The home of the bean and the cod..." – John Collins Bossidy

## Chicken Pot Pie

You might call this upside-down pot pie, because the crust is on top!

*Serves: 4*

*Ingredients:*
1 lb. boneless chicken breast, cubed
1 small, yellow onion, chopped
2 potatoes, diced
1 carrot, peeled and sliced
1 c. frozen peas
2 c. chicken broth
2 T. white flour
1 tube refrigerated rolls – I like crescent rolls for this.
olive oil
1 bay leaf

*Preparation:*
1. Cook the chicken with the onions in 2 T. of oil in a pot. Remove the chicken.
2. Add the potatoes, carrots and peas and sauté 2-3 minutes.
3. Sprinkle the veggies with the flour and mix.
4. Add the chicken broth and simmer for about 10 minutes.
5. When the flour is cooked and the sauce starts to thicken, add back the chicken. You can tell the flour is cooked if it tastes like gravy, not flour.
6. Pull crescent rolls from the tube and make a crust by covering the top with flat pieces. They don't need to be stuck together to make a proper crust – pieces are fine.
7. Cover the pot and cook about 20 minutes, until the rolls are done.

"There is nothing better on a cold, wintry day than a properly made pot pie."
– Craig Claiborne

## Oxtail Stew

This is really for the grownups, though some kids (the smart ones!) like it. Put the pot on as soon as you start the fire in the evening and cook it until after the kids go to bed. Then have your stew with a glass of wine by the fire. That's what camping's all about, Charlie Brown.

*Serves: 4*

*Ingredients:*
6 strips bacon
2 lb. sliced oxtail – see TIP at the bottom.
1 small, yellow onion, chopped
4 carrots, peeled and sliced
2 potatoes, cubed
10 oz. white mushrooms, sliced
1 c. beef broth
½ c. red wine
olive oil
½ c. white flour
salt & pepper
large Ziploc bag

*Preparation:*
1. Cook the bacon in the bottom of a big pot. Feed the bacon to the children. Fight off the stray dogs.
2. In a large, Ziploc bag, put the flour and 1 t. each of salt & pepper. Add the oxtails in batches and get a kid to shake it around.
3. In batches, cook the oxtails in the bacon fat for about 10 minutes.
4. To the braised oxtails, add the beef broth and the wine. Cover and simmer for an hour or longer.
5. Add the onions, carrots, potatoes and mushrooms and simmer another 30 minutes or so.
6. Serve with fresh biscuits and butter and a big glass of red wine.

*TIP:*
- Oxtails can usually be found pre-sliced and packaged in the meat section of a supermarket. The best thing to do, though, is to find a butcher who carries it fresh and ask to have it sliced there.

"If you were plowing a field, which would you rather use? Two strong oxen or 1024 chickens?" – Seymore Cray

MAGGIE DA SILVA

## Veggie Stew

A nice stew for day 4 or 5. Serve it with quesadillas on the side for the kids.

*Serves: 4*

*Ingredients:*
1 small, yellow onion, chopped
2 gloves garlic, minced
2 potatoes, chopped
1 sweet potato, chopped
3 carrots, peeled and sliced
2 parsnips, sliced
2 ears corn, broken into halves
olive oil
salt & pepper and hot sauce
1 bay leaf
1 c. beef broth (or vegetable broth to make this a vegetarian dish)
1 c. shredded Mozzerella or Jack cheese (or soy or rice cheese to make this a vegan dish)

*Preparation:*
1. Cook the onions and garlic in 1 T. of oil in a pot until soft, being careful to not burn the garlic.
2. Add the rest of the vegetables, the bay leaf and the broth.
3. Simmer for about 15 minutes, or until the potatoes and parsnips are cooked. Season with salt & pepper.
4. Serve with shredded cheese, salt & pepper and hot sauce.

*Variation:*
- Add fresh veggies, like yellow or green squash and peppers of all colors.

"The greatest delight the fields and woods minister is the suggestion of an occult relation between man and the vegetable. 'I am not alone and unacknowledged.' They nod to me and I to them." – Ralph Waldo Emerson

## Curried Rice and Beef

This recipe combines two kid favorites, curry powder and rice.

*Serves: 4*

*Ingredients:*
1 lb. hamburger
1 small, yellow onion, chopped
1 c. white rice
3 T. curry powder
2 c. beef broth
olive oil
mango chutney (my favorite)

*Preparation:*
1. Cook the meat and onions in 2 T. of oil in a pot until the meat is cooked.
2. Add the rice and curry powder and sauté for 1 minute.
3. Add the broth and simmer for about 20 minutes, until the rice is done.
4. Serve with mango chutney.

*Variations:*
- Substitute chicken or stew meat for ground beef.
- Substitute a cup of light coconut milk for a cup of beef broth.

"Mark Darcy: I realize that when I met you at the turkey curry buffet, I was unforgivably rude, and wearing a reindeer jumper." – *Bridget Jones's Diary*

## Stew in a Can

You must have your food cooked in a coffee can at least one night when you're camping. That's what the Scouts do.

*Serves: 1*

*Ingredients:*
1 boneless, thin cut porkchop
1 carrot, peeled and sliced
1 small potato, sliced
¼ small, yellow onion, chopped
½ c. beef broth
olive oil
1 nice, clean coffee can

*Preparation:*
1. Put about 1 T. of oil in the bottom of your can.
2. Brown your pork chop in your can over the campfire or on the grill.
3. Add the carrots, potatoes, onions and broth.
4. Cover your can with foil and set it among the coals for 20-30 minutes. Check it often.
5. Enjoy roughing it!

*Variations:*
- Try this with bacon, stew meat, hamburger or chicken.
- Try a vegetarian version with root veggies and cheese on top.

"To poke a wood fire is more solid enjoyment than almost anything else in the world." – Charles Dudley Warner

## Chicken and Rice

This is a nice dish if you don't want to fuss too much with the meal, or you have some leftover chicken to use up.

*Serves: 4*

*Ingredients:*
1 lb. boneless chicken breast, cubed
1 c. white rice
½ small, yellow onion, chopped
1 clove garlic, minced
1 c. frozen carrots & peas
2 c. chicken broth
olive oil
salt & pepper and hot sauce

*Preparation:*
1. Sauté the onions and garlic in a pot with 1 T. olive oil until the onions are soft, being careful to not burn the garlic.
2. Add the chicken, rice and veggies and sauté for 2 minutes.
3. Add the broth and bring the rice to a simmer.
4. Cover the pot and simmer until the rice is done, about 20 minutes.
5. Serve with salt & pepper and hot sauce.

"Poultry is for cookery what canvas is for painting." – Jean-Anthelme Brillat-Savarin

## Chicken and Stuffing

Any excuse to eat stuffing. Am I right?

*Serves: 4*

*Ingredients:*
1 lb. cooked boneless chicken breast, cubed
1 box Stove Top Stuffing or similar
½ small, yellow onion, chopped
1 stalk celery, chopped
1 ½ c. low sodium chicken broth – stuffing mix has plenty of salt in it already.

*Preparation:*
1. Heat the chicken broth with the onion and celery. Simmer for 2 minutes.
2. Add the chicken and bring back to a simmer. Remove the pot from the heat.
3. Add the stuffing and stir well. Cover the pot and let sit for 5 minutes.
4. Yum.

*Variations:*
- Add or substitute bacon, sausage or oysters.
- Try different veggies with this, like carrots, green beans, artichoke hearts, etc.

"No more turkey, but I'd like another helping of that bread he ate."
– Anonymous child, quoted in *Joy of Cooking*

## Goulash!

One of the most delicious things in the world, topped with sour cream. What could be better than that?

*Serves: 4-6*

*Ingredients:*
1 lb. sirloin tips, cubed
1 small, yellow onion, chopped
¼ green pepper, chopped
10 oz. white mushrooms, sliced
2 c. beef broth
2 T. white flour
olive oil
10 oz. wide egg noodles, cooked
1 T. paprika
sour cream
salt & pepper and hot sauce

*Preparation:*
1. Brown the sirloin tips and onions in 1 T. of olive oil in a pot.
2. Add the mushrooms, green pepper and paprika and sauté for 3 minutes.
3. Sprinkle the meat and veggies with flour and stir well.
4. Add the beef broth and bring to a simmer, stirring.
5. Simmer about 40 minutes, until the beef is tender and the broth is thickened.
6. Serve with noodles, a dollop of sour cream, hot sauce and salt & pepper.

"If we were to promise people nothing better than only revolution, they would scratch their heads and say: 'Is it not better to have good goulash?'"
– Nikita Khrushchev

## Chicken and Bacon

Bacon and cheese reunite here for a good cause.

*Serves: 4*

*Ingredients:*
1 lb. boneless chicken breast, cubed
8 strips bacon
½ small, yellow onion, chopped
¼ green pepper, chopped
8 oz. Mozzarella cheese, shredded
salt & pepper and hot sauce

*Preparation:*
1. Cook the bacon and set it aside. Wipe some of the fat out of the skillet.
2. Sauté the chicken in the bacon fat with the onion and pepper until the chicken is cooked, about 5 minutes.
3. Add back the bacon and combine it well.
4. Sprinkle the dish with cheese and cover it. Heat until melted.

*TIP:*
- If you don't want to wash cheese out of your skillet, make this in an aluminum pie plate.

"Life expectancy would grow by leaps and bounds if green vegetables smelled as good as bacon." – Doug Larson

**Stuffed Peppers**

We make these at home and store (or freeze) them in an aluminum foil tray. Then they go right on the grill in the tray once they're defrosted.

*Serves: 4*

*Ingredients:*
4 large bell peppers
1 small, yellow onion, chopped
1 lb. hamburger or ground dark meat turkey
1 c. cooked rice
1 jar tomato sauce
oregano
cumin
salt & pepper

*Preparation:*
1. Sauté the beef with the onion until browned. Season with cumin, oregano and salt & pepper.
2. Add the rice and enough tomato sauce to moisten.
3. Cut tops the off of the peppers (keep the tops) and scoop out insides.
4. Stuff the peppers with the rice and meat mixture and arrange them in an aluminum foil tray. Put the tops back on the peppers.
5. Pour some tomato sauce into the tray to keep the peppers from burning.
6. Cover the tray with foil and place it on a hot grill or directly on medium-hot coals. Cook it about 60 minutes.
7. Serve with hot sauce or Parmesan cheese for the kids.

*Variations:*
- Double wrap each pepper individually in foil and place it directly on the coals.
- Instead of tomato sauce, add 2 beaten eggs to the mixture before stuffing the peppers. Keep the peppers from burning on the bottom by adding a little chicken or beef broth.
- Top the peppers with breadcrumbs and grated cheese before cooking.

"Food for thought is no substitute for the real thing." – Walt Kelly

## Jambalaya

One of my favorite dishes either at home or camping. We make it mild so the kids can eat it, then douse ours with hot sauce.

*Serves: 4*

*Ingredients:*
1 small, yellow onion, minced
1 c. white rice
¼ green pepper, chopped
1 clove garlic, minced
2 or three stems scallions, chopped
1 lb. Italian sausage or Kielbasa
1 lb. chicken thighs on the bone
2 c. chicken broth
salt & pepper and hot sauce

*Preparation:*
1. In a big pot, brown the sausages and the chicken in a little olive oil or bacon fat for about 5 minutes, then set aside.
2. When the sausages cool, slice them.
3. In the same pot, cook the onions and garlic until they are very soft, bring careful to not burn the garlic. Add a little broth or water if necessary.
4. Add the sausage and chicken with the chicken broth and simmer for 15 minutes.
5. Stir in the peppers, scallions and rice.
6. Simmer the rice for 15 minutes, or until the broth is almost absorbed.
7. With a big spoon or spatula, turn the rice over. Move the pot to low heat and keep it there until all the broth is evaporated and rice is done.
8. Serve with salt & pepper and hot sauce.

*Variations:*
- Add cleaned shrimp with their tails removed, or some fresh fish if you have it – filleted and cut into bite-sized pieces first.
- Add a can of tomatoes or a chopped tomato.

"Jambalaya, a-crawfish pie and-a file gumbo
'Cause tonight I'm gonna see my ma cher amio
Pick guitar, fill fruit jar and be gay-oh
Son of a gun, we'll have big fun on the bayou."
– Hank Williams, Jr.

## Dutch Oven Pizza

More fun for the kids, and it's tasty, too

*Serves: 2, so plan to make it twice in a row, or make another one on the grill.*

*Ingredients:*
½ lb. refrigerated pizza dough
½ jar marinara sauce
¾ lb. Mozzarella cheese, shredded
½ lb. Pepperoni or cooked sausage, sliced
1 aluminum pie tin
spray cooking oil

*Preparation:*
1. Spray the pie tin with spray cooking oil.
2. Spread the dough inside the pie tin.
3. Top the dough with the sauce, cheese and meat.
4. Put some pebbles or gravel in the bottom of the Dutch Oven to raise the pie tin off the bottom.
5. Set the pie tin on the gravel.
6. Cover the Dutch Oven. Set it in the coals and shovel some coals on top.
7. Cook for approx 20 minutes. (Check often.)

*Variations:*
- Instead of pizza dough, line the bottom of the Dutch Oven with hamburger rolls or any kind of bread. No pie tin needed.
- Add sautéed spinach or mushrooms under the cheese. Try olives, broccoli, onions, etc.
- Doctor the sauce for a more homemade flavor: Sauté the minced onions and garlic in olive oil, add some chopped green peppers and cook until soft. Then add sauce and bring to a simmer.

"You better cut the pizza in four pieces because I'm not hungry enough to eat six." – Yogi Berra

# SEAFOOD

### Fish in the Pan by Pete

This is Pete's tried-and-true fish recipe. He says, "For cooking a mess of fish when you're camping start with a large cast iron pan and a stick of butter."

*Serves: 4*

*Ingredients:*
2-4 lbs. whole fish, cleaned, gutted and scaled
1 c. white or whole wheat flour
Lawry's seasoned salt
Butter
Hot sauce

*Preparation:*
1. Scale, gut and clean your fish. Remove the head.
2. Put 1 c. of flour and 2 T. of Lawry's seasoned salt in a Ziploc bag. Add the cleaned fish and shake well.
3. Heat a skillet over the fire and put the whole stick of butter in once the pan is hot.
4. When the butter melts, lay in the fish.
5. Cook for 2-3 minutes on each side.
6. Serve with hot sauce.

*Variations:*
- Try cornmeal instead of flour for a crunchy coating.
- You can also cook this on the fire in a foil pack – just put the fish and a big pat of butter in the foil pack and seal – cook it directly on medium coals or on a hot grill.

"In the hands of an able cook, fish can become an inexhaustible source of perpetual delight." – Jean-Anthelme Brillat-Savarin

## Oyster Po' Boys

Easy to make, strictly for the grownups and for our one child who likes to eat slimy things.

*Serves: 2*

*Ingredients:*
1 16 oz. jar fresh, shucked oysters
½ c. white or whole wheat flour
1 T. Lawry's seasoned salt
olive oil
hero rolls (or hamburger buns)
tartar sauce
salt & pepper and hot sauce

*Preparation:*
1. Combine flour and Lawry's seasoning in a Ziploc bag.
2. Heat about 2 T. of oil in a skillet to hot but not smoking.
3. Shake the oysters in the flour mixture and fry in the skillet until golden brown.
4. Drain the oysters on paper towels to absorb the oil.
5. Toast the rolls on the grill. Slather both sides with tartar sauce.
6. Fill the rolls with oysters, around 6 per roll.
7. Serve with salt & pepper, hot sauce and more tartar sauce.

*Variations:*
- You can also use raw, cleaned and peeled shrimp.
- This is extra nice with lettuce and tomato, if you have any.

---

"A loaf of bread, the Walrus said,
Is what we chiefly need:
Pepper and vinegar besides
Are very good indeed--
Now if you're ready, Oysters, dear,
We can begin to feed!"
– Lewis Carroll, *Alice Through the Looking-Glass*

## Fish Tacos by Pete

Pete says, "The more sauce the better."

*Serves: 4*

*Ingredients:*
2 lbs. fish, cleaned and fileted
butter
corn tortillas
½ head cabbage, chopped
sauce: mayonnaise, water, white onion, cilantro, salt & pepper
lime or lemon wedges
hot sauce

*Preparation:*
1. Fry the fish in butter and season it with salt & pepper.
2. Chop the cabbage thinly.
3. Warm the tortillas on the grill and stack them – stacking keeps them warm.
4. Make the sauce: Mix equal parts of mayonnaise and water, add 2–3 T. chopped onion, some chopped cilantro and salt & pepper. We usually make about a cup of sauce.
5. Place a fish filet or two into a warm tortilla. Sprinkle in chopped cabbage, and spoon in some sauce.
6. Serve with lime or lemon wedges, hot sauce and salt & pepper.

"Most seafoods...should be simply threatened with heat and then celebrated with joy." – Jeff Smith (The Frugal Gourmet)

## Stuffed fish

Another good reason to eat stuffing.

*Serves: 4*

*Ingredients:*
2-4 lbs. fish, cleaned, gutted and scaled, but with head and tail left on.
Stove Top stuffing or similar
olive oil
lemon wedges
salt & pepper and hot sauce

*Preparation:*
1. Make the stuffing according to the directions on the package.
2. Lay out a double thickness of foil per fish, and oil the inside liberally.
3. Place the fish on the foil and stuff the inside cavity of the fish with stuffing.
4. Wrap the fish up in the foil and place it on the hot grill.
5. Cook about 30 minutes.
6. Serve with lemon wedges, hot sauce, salt & pepper

*Variations:*
- Omit the stuffing and fill the fish with onions, cilantro, garlic and lemon.
- Wrap the fish in a couple of strips of bacon before wrapping it in foil.

"Don't tell fish stories where the people know you; but particularly, don't tell them where they know the fish." – Mark Twain

## Grilled Shrimp

These cook super fast, so you can snack on them while the rest of the dinner cooks. Or you can serve these as an entrée over rice.

*Serves: 2-4*

*Ingredients:*
1 lb. raw shrimp, cleaned and deveined, but with the tails left on
1 stick butter, melted
1 clove garlic, minced
metal skewers

*Preparation:*
1. Skewer the shrimp on the skewers.
2. Mix the melted butter with the garlic on a plate.
3. Dip the skewers in garlic butter and place them on the grill.
4. Cook about 2 minutes on each side and remove from the grill.
5. Let the skewers cool down a bit, then serve on the skewer.

*Variations:*
- Marinate the shrimp in olive oil and Lawry's seasoned salt instead of butter and garlic.

"Eat butter first, and eat it last, and live till a hundred years be past." – Old Dutch proverb

## Dutch Oven Shrimp and Sausages

So easy and you can serve it over rice or with biscuits, whichever you like.

*Serves: 4*

*Ingredients:*
1 lb. raw shrimp, cleaned and deveined, but with the tails left on
1 lb. Italian sausage or Kielbasa, sliced
2 ears corn, broken in half to make 4 pieces
2 c. chicken broth

*Preparation:*
1. Place the sliced sausages in the bottom of a Dutch Oven.
2. Lay the shrimp on top of the sausages and the corn on top of the shrimp.
3. Pour in the chicken broth and close the Dutch Oven.
4. Cook on hot coals about 30 minutes, until the sausages are done.
5. Serve with rice or biscuits.

"First we eat, then we do everything else." – M. F. K. Fisher

# BONUS CHICKEN RECIPES

## Chicken Cordon Bleu

So easy. So French.

*Serves: 2-4*

*Ingredients:*
2 boneless chicken breasts sliced lengthways to make 4 pieces
4 slices ham
4 slices Swiss cheese
¾ c. white or whole wheat flour
salt & pepper
olive oil
butter
aluminum foil

*Preparation:*
1. Tear off a rectangle of aluminum foil and fold it in half to make a double thick square. Oil the inside of the foil well.
2. In a Ziploc bag, mix the flour with 1 t. each of salt and pepper.
3. Take one piece of chicken and lay it flat.
4. Put one piece of ham and one piece of cheese on the chicken.
5. Roll it up and dredge it in the flour mixture. Secure it with a toothpick.
6. Shake the chicken gently in flour and shake off the excess flour.
7. Wrap the chicken up in the foil, snugly but not too tightly.
8. Cook it on a hot grill turning often, for about 25 minutes.
9. Serve with salt & pepper.

*Variation:*
- Substitute cream cheese for Swiss cheese.

"You Banbury cheese!" – William Shakespeare, *The Merry Wives of Windsor*

## Chicken Fingers

I'm not sure why kids like their food shaped like fingers, but they do.

*Serves: 4*

*Ingredients:*
1 lb. boneless chicken breast, cut into strips
olive oil
salt & pepper, hot sauce and BBQ sauce
metal skewers

*Preparation:*
1. Thread the chicken strips onto skewers.
2. Pour ½ c. of olive oil onto a plate.
3. Roll the chicken skewers in the oil.
4. Salt and pepper the skewers and grill them over medium coals.
5. Serve with salt & pepper, hot sauce and BBQ sauce
6. Kids like pita bread with this.

"I love chicken. I would eat chicken fingers on Thanksgiving if it were socially acceptable." – Todd Barry

## Chicken Fingers II

An easy breezy variation.

*Serves: 4*

*Ingredients:*
1 lb. skinless, boneless chicken breast, cut into strips
1 egg, beaten
1 c. prepared breadcrumbs
¼ c. Parmesan cheese, grated
olive oil
aluminum foil
catsup and hot sauce

*Preparation:*
1. Beat the egg by cracking it into a Ziploc bag and letting the kids squish it around.
2. Mix the breadcrumbs and Parmesan cheese in another Ziploc bag.
3. Lay a sheet of aluminum foil on the grill and coat with olive oil.
4. Dip each piece of chicken in the egg bag, then the crumbs bag, then lay it on the foil.
5. Cook over a hot fire 3-5 minutes per side.
6. Serve with catsup, and hot sauce for the grownups.

"Left wing, chicken wing, it don't make no difference to me." – Woody Guthrie

## Satay Chicken

Prep this at home the night before you go, then just pop it on the grill.

*Serves: 4*

*Ingredients:*

Chicken
1 lb. skinless, boneless chicken breast
½ medium onion, chopped
½ c. soy sauce
1 T. chopped garlic or 1 t. garlic powder
1 T. peanut oil
1 T. brown sugar
wooden skewers

Dipping Sauce
¾ c. smooth peanut butter
¼ c. soy sauce
1 T. brown sugar juice
1 lime
hot water

*Preparation:*
1. Mix together the onion, ½ c. soy sauce, garlic, peanut oil and 1 T. brown sugar in a large Ziploc bag.
2. Slice the chicken into strips.
3. Thread each chicken strip onto a skewer. Put all the chicken skewers in the Ziploc bag of marinade and marinate - for several hours if you can.
4. In a blender, combine the peanut butter, ¼ c. soy sauce, lime juice and the remaining 1 T. brown sugar.
5. While it's blending, drizzle in about ¼ c. hot water, give or take. The sauce should be the consistency of drippy pancake batter.
6. Put the peanut sauce in a jar and refrigerate.
7. At the campsite, either grill the chicken skewers directly on the grill or place a piece of aluminum foil down and grill the chicken on that.
8. Stir the peanut sauce and let the kids dip directly into the jar.
9. Extremely yummy.

"The discovery of a new dish does more for human happiness than the discovery of a star." – Anthelme Brillat-Savarin

MAGGIE DA SILVA

## Lemon Chicken

For the grownups.

*Serves: 4*

*Ingredients:*
4 chicken breasts
½ c. olive oil
juice of 2 lemons
1 clove garlic, minced
1 t. oregano
salt & pepper

*Preparation:*
1. In a Ziploc bag, combine the olive oil, lemon juice, garlic, oregano and ½ t. each of salt & pepper.
2. Add the chicken and marinate for at least 15 minutes.
3. Grill over hot coals for about 20 minutes, turning often and basting with the marinade.
4. Serve with rice.

"I believe that if life gives you lemons, you should make lemonade... And try to find somebody whose life has given them vodka, and have a party." – Ron White

## Peanut Butter Chicken

We make this at home, too. Always popular with the youth.

*Serves: 4*

*Ingredients:*
1 ½ lb. boneless chicken breast, cut into bite-sized pieces
1/3 c. peanut butter
1 T. brown sugar
2 T. soy sauce
1 clove garlic, minced
1 T. catsup
salt & pepper

*Preparation:*
1. Put the peanut butter, sugar, soy sauce, garlic, catsup and ½ t. each salt & pepper into a large Ziploc bag. Seal and have the children smush it around to mix it up.
2. Place the chicken in the Ziploc bag with the marinade. Have the children smush it around to mix it.
3. Cook the chicken in a skillet or in foil on the grill. Add enough marinade to keep each piece well-coated.
4. Serve with noodles or rice.

"Peanut butter is the paté of childhood." – Florence Fabricant

MAGGIE DA SILVA

# BREADS AND DESSERTS

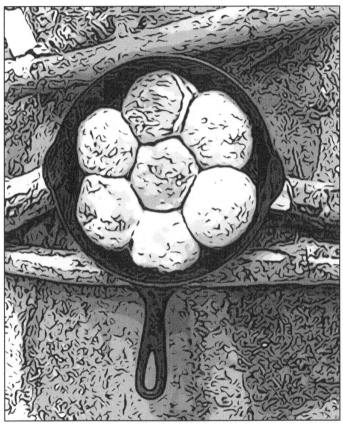

*Monkey Bread*

MAGGIE DA SILVA

# BREADS

**Bread on a Stick**

A camping classic. Sometimes we have it every day!

*Feeds: 4-6*

*Ingredients:*
1 tube refrigerated biscuit dough
1 green, pointy stick

*Preparation:*
1. Take a piece of biscuit dough and stretch it into a long, skinny snake.
2. Wrap the dough snake around a long stick and cook it over the fire until it's golden brown.
3. Serve with butter and jam or cinnamon sugar.

"When you're down on your luck and you've lost all your dreams there's nothing like a campfire and a can of beans." – Tom Waits, *Lucky Days*

## Bannock

Bannock (pronounced BAN-nuck) is an old camping classic. It's a flat bread, a lot like Native American Frybread, except it resembles a rock in texture. It's fun to make, and with enough butter, almost edible.

*Serves: 4*

*Ingredients:*
1 c. whole wheat flour
1 t. baking powder
¼ t. salt
water
olive oil

*Preparation:*
1. Combine the dry ingredients in a bowl.
2. Add water little by little until you have a firm dough.
3. Some people knead the dough at this point, but we don't, because it's too hard to keep it clean at the campsite.
4. Cover the bowl with a damp dishtowel or t-shirt and set the bowl near the fire (but not too near) to rise for about 20 minutes.
5. Punch down the dough and make a big patty cake about 1 inch thick that fits into your skillet.
6. Grease the skillet well with olive oil and fry the dough over medium heat until it's golden brown, 5-10 minutes on each side.
7. Serve with butter, honey, brown sugar, peanut butter & jelly. Or just gnaw on a piece while you're sitting around the fire.

*Variations:*
- Instead of water use milk, or add some powdered milk to the flour.
- Add brown sugar, cinnamon and about a handful of raisins and/or nuts to the dough - roll out the dough and spread it with butter and then add the rest. Roll it up and slice into 1" thick slices and fry in a skillet.
- Add honey or a couple of teaspoons of sugar to the dough.
- Instead of cooking it in a frying pan, make some long snakes of dough and wrap them around sticks for the kids to cook over the fire.

*TIP:*
- It takes practice to make a bannock cake that is cooked through but not overcooked. Tap it when you think it's done. If it sounds hollow, it's done.

"Acorns were good until bread was found." – Francis Bacon

## Hardtack (Make at Home)

Hardtack, also known as Sea Biscuit, is a simple, hard cracker that was once a staple of long sea voyages. It's great with chowder.

*Serves: 8*

*Ingredients:*
2 c. yogurt
½ c. honey
½ c. olive oil
6 c. whole wheat flour + extra for rolling
1 t. salt
sesame seeds

*Preparation:*
1. Mix all of the ingredients together and knead until smooth.
2. Roll dough out thin and cut it into 2" crackers. (A pizza cutter is good for this.)
3. Bake the crackers on a cookie sheet at 375 degrees for 10-15 minutes, or until they are just brown.

"Hoist your sail when the wind is fair." – Proverb

## Hudson Bay Bread (Make at Home)

Another classic; the original energy bar. Good for older kids who are canoeing or hiking all day to take along with them.

*Serves: 10*

*Ingredients:*
1 stick butter, softened
2 c. sugar
¼ c. honey
¼ c. maple syrup
½ c. chopped walnuts
8 c. minute oats
1 c. whole wheat flour

*Preparation:*
1. Mix everything together well, except for the nuts, oats and flour.
2. Stir in the nuts, oats and flour.
3. Spread the mixture onto a large jelly roll pan (a cookie sheet with a lip). Press it down until it's less than ½" thick.
4. Bake the bread at 300 degrees for about 15 minutes – it shouldn't get too hard.
5. While it's still warm, cut the bread into bars or squares.
6. Serve instead of bread with peanut butter and jelly.

*Variation:*
- You can substitute molasses for the honey or maple syrup.

"And I had but one penny in the world. Thou should'st have it to buy gingerbread." – William Shakespeare, *Love's Labours Lost*

# DESSERTS

**S'Mores**

Invented by the Girl Scouts.

*Serves: 4*

*Ingredients:*
4 graham crackers
4 marshmallows
2 Hershey's milk chocolate bars
green, pointy sticks

*Preparation:*
1. Toast each marshmallow on a long stick over the fire until it's golden brown.
2. Put a piece of chocolate on a graham cracker and put a hot, roasted marshmallow on top of the chocolate.
3. Cover with a second graham cracker and smush together to make a S'more.
4. Bon appétit!

*Variations:*
- Try with Nutella or different kinds of chocolate. I like peanut butter cups.
- Put some sliced banana or other fruit inside.
- Add some peanut butter inside.
- Try with refrigerated biscuits – stretch one out and put a piece of chocolate and a marshmallow inside. Wrap it in foil and cook it on the grill or directly on the coals.
- Substitute brownies, cookies or cake for the graham crackers.
- Substitute apple slices for the graham crackers, and add peanut butter.
- Use an ice cream cone instead of graham crackers – just put a piece of chocolate and a hot, roasted marshmallow inside.

- Use a tortilla instead of graham crackers – sprinkle a tortilla with chocolate chips and mini marshmallows, roll up and wrap in foil. Place on the grill until melted.
- Make in a sandwich iron with bread instead of graham crackers.
- Simplify – put a marshmallow between 2 chocolate chip cookies, wrap in foil and toss on the fire.

"Life is uncertain. Eat dessert first." – Ernestine Ulmer

## Chocolate Chip Cookies

This recipe is easy, so you might as well make it from scratch.

*Ingredients:*
2 c. flour
2 eggs
1 stick butter, softened
1 c. semi-sweet chocolate chips
1 c. sugar
1 t. vanilla extract
aluminum foil pan or pie plates
aluminum foil

*Preparation:*
1. Mix together the butter, sugar and vanilla until smooth.
2. Beat in the eggs.
3. Gradually mix in the flour until it's evenly combined.
4. Stir in the chocolate chips.
5. Drop the batter by spoonfuls onto the ungreased foil pan or pie plates.
6. Cover the pan with foil and cook it on the grill or in the coals for about 10 minutes.
7. They will all smoosh together, but you can separate them with a spatula.
8. Bon appétit!

*Variation:*
- You can also make this in a Dutch Oven in a pie plate set on top of an upside down pie plate.

"Cookies are made of butter and love." – Norwegian Proverb

## Chocolate Cake Oranges

Fun and tasty, and the kids like to eat the oranges, too.

*Serves: 6*

*Ingredients:*
1 package chocolate cake mix
whatever is needed to make the mix, such as an egg and some oil
6 oranges
aluminum foil

*Preparation:*
1. Slice the tops off of the oranges, scoop out the insides and eat the insides.
2. Make the cake mix according to the directions on the package.
3. Spoon the cake into the oranges to about ¾ of the way full.
4. Put the tops back on the oranges and wrap them in foil.
5. Place the oranges in the coals for about 15 minutes.
6. Eat the cake out of the oranges with spoons.

*Variations:*
- Try with other cake mixes, like yellow or spice cake.
- Try with muffin mix for a breakfast treat. I like blueberry flavored with this.

"And every day when I've been good, I get an orange after food." – Robert Louis Stevenson

## Broom Handle Eclairs

My favorite treat of them all.

*Serves: 6*

*Ingredients:*
1 tube refrigerated crescent roll dough
pre-made vanilla pudding (in the refrigerator section of the supermarket)
chocolate syrup (I like U-bet - it's made in Brooklyn!)
aluminum foil

*Preparation:*
1. Take a piece of crescent roll dough and stretch it around the end of a broom handle until you have a long cup.
2. Toast the cup carefully over the fire until it is golden brown. (You can also make a dough cup around a "stick" of aluminum foil and toast it on a stick.)
3. Fill the middle of the roll with vanilla pudding and drizzle it with chocolate syrup.

*Variations:*
- Fill the éclair with whipped cream or fruit pie filling instead of pudding.
- For a dinner roll, fill the éclair with a pat of butter and let it melt.

"Once in a young lifetime one should be allowed to have as much sweetness as one can possibly want and hold." – Judith Olney

## Brownies

Nobody doesn't like brownies.

*Ingredients:*
1 box brownie mix
whatever is needed to make the mix, such as an egg and some oil
½ c. chocolate chips
butter
aluminum foil pan
aluminum foil

*Preparation:*
1. Butter the aluminum foil pan.
2. Make the cake mix according to the directions on the package.
3. Pour the mixture into the foil pan.
4. Sprinkle with the chocolate chips and cover with foil.
5. Cook on the grill or coals for 30-40 minutes.
6. Check the brownies often with a toothpick – if the toothpick comes out clean, it's done.

*Variation:*
- I like this with peanut butter chips.

"Las cosas claras y el chocolate espeso." (Ideas should be clear and chocolate thick.) – Spanish Proverb

## Fudge

If your kid is a chocolate lover this fudge can be used for currency with her. Either way, it's fun to squish it around.

*Serves: 6*

*Ingredients:*
½ bar of cream cheese
2 c. confectioner's sugar
¼ c. unsweetened cocoa
¼ stick of butter
2 Ziploc bags, 1 gallon size

*Preparation:*
1. Put everything into one of the Ziploc bags, squeeze out the air and zip it tight.
2. Put the full Ziploc bag inside the empty one, squeeze the air out of that Ziploc bag, too.
3. Have the kids squish it around until everything is evenly mixed.
4. Scoop out with a spoon into bowls.

"Fudge is made by chocolate angels." – Alexis F. Hope

## Chocolate Fondue

Delicious and festive.

*Ingredients:*
4 c. semi-sweet chocolate chips
¼ stick of butter
½ c. milk
fruit cut into chunks: apples, bananas, oranges, dried apricots, etc.
wooden skewers or sticks
aluminum foil pie pan

*Preparation:*
1. Put the butter and the chocolate chips into the pie pan on a hot grill and mix together.
2. Mix in the milk with a fork, stirring constantly, until it's blended.
3. Let people choose chunks of fruit, put them on their skewers, and dip them into the chocolate.

*Variations:*
- You can also dip in pieces of cake or muffins, pretzels or popcorn or, of course, marshmallows.
- This can be made with white chocolate or peanut butter chips.
- If you're making this just for the grownups you can mix in a big splash of liqueur, like Kahlua or orange liqueur.

"All I really need is love, but a little chocolate now and then doesn't hurt!"
– Charles Schulz

## Fruit Kebabs

If your kids think grilled fruit is weird, they can just eat the raw fruit off the kebabs; it's still fun.

*Serves: 4*

*Ingredients:*
2 apples, cut into thick slices
2 bananas, cut into 1/2" slices
1 mango, cut into bite-sized pieces
1 box of strawberries, washed
metal or wooden skewers
aluminum foil

*Preparation:*
1. If you use wooden skewers, soak them in water first so they don't burn.
2. Let the kids thread the fruit onto the skewers.
3. Place the skewers on foil on the grill and cook them until the fruit is tender and lightly browned.
4. Serve with chocolate syrup, or just on their own.

"Strawberries are the angels of the earth, innocent and sweet with green leafy wings reaching heavenward." – Terri Guillemets

## Pie Iron Apple Pie

Grownups like this fresh-tasting and not too sweet dessert.

*Serves: 1*

*Ingredients:*
2 slices bread
½ apple, thinly sliced
butter
brown sugar
cinnamon

*Preparation:*
1. Butter both sides of 2 slices of bread, and place them in the pie iron.
2. In the middle of the bread, lay some sliced apples, brown sugar, cinnamon and a pat of butter.
3. Close the pie iron and hold it over medium coals for about 5 minutes. Don't let the butter burn.

*Variations:*
- Use canned pie filling, and try different flavors. Cherry is yummy.
- Try with cream cheese and cinnamon sugar.
- Use biscuit dough instead of bread – butter the iron first.

"If you want to make an apple pie from scratch, you must first create the universe." – Carl Sagan

## Fried Cherry Pie

The problem with these is that once you start eating them you don't want to eat anything else the whole trip.

*Serves: 6*

*Ingredients:*
1 tube refrigerated biscuit dough
1 can cherry pie filling
butter

*Preparation:*
1. Take a biscuit and flatten it out with your fingers.
2. Spoon filling into the center of the dough, fold it over and crimp the edges with a fork.
3. Fry the pie in butter in a skillet over low heat until it's done, about 5 minutes on each side.
4. Remove the pie from the skillet and sprinkle it with sugar.
5. Wait 5-10 minutes for the pie to cool down. Cherry filling is hot!

*Variation:*
- Try with apple or peach pie filling and cinnamon sugar on top. Mmm.

"One must ask children and birds how cherries and strawberries taste."
– Johann Wolfgang von Goethe

## Applesauce Cake

Weird, fun and yummy.

*Serves: 6*

*Ingredients:*
1 jar applesauce
1 package cake mix, such as spice, gingerbread or yellow cake
aluminum foil pan
aluminum foil

*Preparation:*
1. Pour the applesauce in the bottom of the pan.
2. Pour the dry cake mix evenly over the applesauce.
3. Cover the pan with foil and place it on the grill.
4. Cook the concoction until the applesauce has steamed the cake mix into a cake, 30-45 minutes.
5. Serve warm.

*Variation:*
- This works well in a Dutch Oven, as well. You can also cook it in clean, buttered coffee cans.

"What a healthy out-of-door appetite it takes to relish the apple of life, the apple of the world, then!" – Henry David Thoreau, *Wild Apples*

## Apple Crisp

I could eat the whole pan. Admit it, you could too.

*Serves: 6*

*Ingredients:*
6 apples, peeled and sliced
½ stick butter
½ c. brown sugar
1 c. flour
4 packets plain instant oatmeal or ½ c. of quick oats
1 T. cinnamon
aluminum foil pan
aluminum foil

*Preparation:*
1. Put the apple slices into an aluminum pan.
2. Mix together the sugar, flour, oats and cinnamon. Sprinkle the mixture over the apples.
3. Cut the butter into pieces and scatter them over the top of the mixture.
4. Cover the crisp with foil and cook it on the grill for about 45 minutes, until the apples are soft.

"But I, when I undress me
Each night, upon my knees
Will ask the Lord to bless me
With apple-pie and cheese. " – Eugene Field

## Baked Apples

Easy and cozy.

*Serves: 1*

*Ingredients:*
1 apple
1 T. raisins
1 T. chopped walnuts
1 T. brown sugar
½ t. cinnamon
1 pat butter
aluminum foil

*Preparation:*
1. Core the apple, but don't cut it all the way through to the bottom.
2. Stuff the center with the raisins, walnuts, cinnamon & brown sugar.
3. Top it with a pat of butter.
4. Wrap the apple in a double thickness of foil and cook it on the coals for about 20 minutes.
5. Open the foil and let the apple cool before eating it with a spoon.

*Variation:*
- Try this with maple syrup instead of brown sugar. Or both.

"Good apple pies are a considerable part of our domestic happiness." – Jane Austen

## Caramel Crisp Apples

Crunchy, butterscotchy, yummy.

*Serves: 1*

*Ingredients:*
1 apple
1 T. brown sugar
1 T. flour
1 T. quick oats or instant oatmeal
½ t. cinnamon
1 T. butterscotch chips
1 pat butter
aluminum foil

*Preparation:*
1. Core the apple, but don't cut it all the way through to the bottom.
2. Stuff the center with the brown sugar, flour, oats, cinnamon and butterscotch chips.
3. Top it with a pat of butter.
4. Wrap the apple in a double thickness of foil and cook it on the coals for about 20 minutes.
5. Open the foil and let the apple cool before eating it with a spoon.

"Woke up, it was a Chelsea morning, and the first thing that I knew
There was milk and toast and honey and a bowl of oranges, too.
And the sun poured in like butterscotch and stuck to all my senses."
– Joni Mitchell, *Chelsea Morning*

## Fried Apples

These are nice for breakfast.

*Serves: 4*

*Ingredients:*
2 apples, peeled, cored and sliced thinly into rounds
½ c. flour
1 egg
¼ c. milk
butter
sugar
cinnamon

*Preparation:*
1. In a skillet, melt 1 T. of butter.
2. Beat together the egg and the milk, and mix in the melted butter once it's cooled.
3. Mix in the flour, 2 t. of sugar and 1 t. of cinnamon. Beat well, until smooth.
4. In the skillet, melt another 1 T. of butter.
5. Dip the apple slices in the batter and fry them in the skillet, over medium heat.
6. When browned (after about 2 minutes) turn the slices over and cook them on the other side.
7. Drain the cooked apple slices on paper towels and sprinkle with cinnamon sugar.

*Variation:*
- Serve with maple syrup, or sprinkle with confectioner's sugar.

"Thy breath is like the steame of apple-pyes." – Robert Greene, *Arcadia* (1590) – The first written mention of a fruit pie

## Peach Cobbler

Easy, fun and so darned delicious.

*Serves: 4–6*

*Ingredients:*
2 large cans cling peaches, in juice.
Bisquick
cinnamon
sugar

*Preparation:*
1. Open the cans of peaches and save the tops of the cans.
2. Drain off the juice and reserve it. Leave the peaches in the cans.
3. Mix about 1 c. of Bisquick with about ½ c. of juice, to make a batter.
4. Sprinkle the peaches with 1 t. each cinnamon and sugar.
5. Pour the batter over the peaches in the cans.
6. Put the tops of the cans back on, and set the cans in the hot coals.
7. Cook until the batter is brown on top, about 15 minutes.

"The ripest peach is highest on the tree." – James Whitcomb Riley

## Peach "Pie"

Can't wait for the pie to cook? Me neither.

*Serves: 4*

*Ingredients:*
graham crackers
1 can cling peaches in juice
whipped cream
cinnamon

*Preparation:*
1. Put a graham cracker on a plate and top it with a dollop of whipped cream.
2. Add a couple of peach slices and a sprinkle of cinnamon.
3. Top with another dollop of whipped cream and another graham cracker.
4. Squish the sandwich together. Bon appétit!

"Life is better than death, I believe, if only because it is less boring and because it has fresh peaches in it." – Thomas Walker

## Sweet Potato Pie

Fun and easy to make at the campsite.

*Serves: 8*

*Ingredients:*
4 sweet potatoes
1 stick butter
1 egg
½ c. milk
¾ c. sugar
1 t. pumpkin pie spice or cinnamon
½ t. salt
9" pie crust
aluminum foil

*Preparation:*
1. Wash the sweet potatoes thoroughly (at home), wrap them in aluminum foil and cook them in the coals of the fire for 30-45 minutes, checking often. (Or cook them at home, like we do!)
2. Remove the potatoes from the fire, scoop out the insides and mash them with the butter. Cool.
3. Add the egg, milk, sugar, spices and salt and mix well, until smooth.
4. Spoon the mixture into the pie crust.
5. Cover the pie with aluminum foil to keep out ashes, etc. and cook it on the grill for about 1 hour.
6. Cool.
7. Goes well with roasted marshmallows!

"Once you get a spice in your home, you have it forever. Women never throw out spices. The Egyptians were buried with their spices. I know which one I'm taking with me when I go." – Erma Bombeck

## Roasted Bananas

Gooey and sweet, sweet, sweet!

*Serves: 4*

*Ingredients:*
4 bananas
½ c. mini-marshmallows
½ c. semi-sweet chocolate chips
½ c. walnuts, chopped
aluminum foil

*Preparation:*
1. Peel the bananas and reserve the peels.
2. Slice each banana in half and sprinkle each one with marshmallows, chips and walnuts.
3. Close each banana up in its own skin and wrap it tightly in foil.
4. Place the bananas on the grill or directly on the coals for 5-10 minutes.
5. Let the bananas cool a bit before you unwrap them.
6. Eat them with spoons.

*Variation:*
- Try these with peanut butter and/or jelly.

"Yeah, I like cars and basketball. But you know what I like more? Bananas." – Frankie Muniz

## Banana Pies

The graham cracker crust is key.

*Serves: 4*

*Ingredients:*
4 mini graham cracker pie crusts
2 bananas
½ c. peanut butter
2 Hershey's milk chocolate bars
4 marshmallows
aluminum foil pan
aluminum foil

*Preparation:*
1. Layer the bottom of each pie crust with sliced bananas.
2. Put a dollop of peanut butter on top of the bananas.
3. Top the peanut butter with a square of chocolate.
4. Top the chocolate with a marshmallow.
5. Squish it all down as much as possible.
6. Put the pies on an aluminum pan and cover it with foil.
7. Cook them on the grill for about 15 minutes, until everything is melted and hot.
8. Serve with spoons.

"Time flies like an arrow; fruit flies like a banana." – Groucho Marx

## Banana Coffee Cake

We always use muffin mix when we're camping. It's easier and more fun.

*Serves: 4-6*

*Ingredients:*
1 box muffin mix, I like bran with this
whatever is needed to make the mix, such as an egg and some oil
2 bananas
½ c. brown sugar
butter
aluminum foil or a skillet cover

*Preparation:*
1. Butter a skillet all the way up the sides.
2. Make the muffin mix according to the directions on the package and pour it into skillet.
3. Slice bananas and place them on top of the batter.
4. Crumble brown sugar over the bananas (you can use less than ½ cup. I just like brown sugar a lot).
5. Dot the top with butter.
6. Cover the skillet and cook it on medium heat for 20-30 minutes.

*Variation:*
- Sprinkle nuts on top.

"Sometimes I've believed as many as six impossible things before breakfast." – Lewis Carroll, *Alice in Wonderland*

## Pineapple Rings

Easy and fun.

*Ingredients:*
1 can pineapple slices in juice
marshmallows
green, pointy sticks

*Preparation:*
1. Put a marshmallow into a pineapple slice hole and work a pointy stick through the whole thing (it goes through the pineapple slice twice).
2. Toast over a low fire until the pineapple is hot and the marshmallow is toasted.
3. Serve with plates.

"He'll be marshmallows in 5 seconds!" – *Willy Wonka & the Chocolate Factory*

## Pineapple Upside Down Cake

One of my favorite desserts, and it's easy.

*Ingredients:*
1 box yellow cake mix
whatever is needed to make the mix, such as an egg and some oil
1 can pineapple slices
½ c. brown sugar
butter
aluminum foil pan
aluminum foil

*Preparation:*
1. Make the cake mix according to the directions on the package.
2. Put the aluminum pan on the grill and melt about 3 T. of butter in it.
3. Sprinkle brown sugar into the butter.
4. Lay pineapple slices on the bottom of the pan, covering it.
5. Pour the cake batter over the pineapple slices.
6. Cover the pan with aluminum foil and cook it on the grill for 30-40 minutes.
7. Test with a toothpick – if it comes out clean, the cake is done.
8. Turn each slice upside down as you serve it on plates, so the pineapple slice is on top.

*Variations:*
- This cooks well in a Dutch Oven, also.
- Individual cakes – split a donut or muffin in half and put a pineapple slice on one of the halves. Add a spoonful of brown sugar and a pat of butter and put the other half on top. Wrap it in foil and cook it on the grill or in the coals. Mmm.

"He is the very pineapple of politeness!" – Richard Brinsley Sheridan

## Cherry Cake

Even better.

*Ingredients:*
1 box yellow cake mix
whatever is needed to make the mix, such as an egg and some oil
1 can cherries, or cherry pie filling
1 stick butter
aluminum foil pan
aluminum foil

*Preparation:*
1. Melt the stick of butter in an aluminum pan on the grill.
2. Make the cake mix according to the directions on the package.
3. When the butter is sizzling, pour the cake batter into the pan.
4. Then pour the can of cherries or cherry filling right into the center of the batter.
5. Cover the pan with aluminum foil and cook it on the grill for 30-40 minutes.
6. Test it with a toothpick – if it comes out clean, the cake is done.

Variation:
- This cooks well in a Dutch Oven, too.

"Don't give cherries to pigs or advice to fools." – Irish saying

## Craisy Cakes

When you eat these, you have to say, "These cakes are craisy!" at least once.

*Serves: 4-6*

*Ingredients:*
1 box muffin mix, I like corn with this.
whatever is needed to make the mix, such as an egg and some oil
¼ c. brown sugar
¼ c. Craisins (dried, sweetened cranberries) or raisins
spray oil
aluminum foil

*Preparation:*
1. Make little cups out of aluminum foil and spray the insides of the cups with spray oil. Make little covers, too.
2. Make the muffin mix according to the directions on the package.
3. Stir in the cranberries or raisins.
4. Pour the batter into the foil cups.
5. Cover the cups with the little foil covers and bake them over medium heat for 5 minutes.
6. Open the tops, sprinkle the cakes with brown sugar, close them back up and bake them for 10 more minutes, until done.

*Variation:*
- Make one large cake in a skillet instead.

"Eat breakfast like a king, lunch like a prince and dinner like a pauper."
– Adelle Davis

## Bread Pudding

My best friend's Mom's favorite dessert. This is for Manya.

*Serves: 4-6*

*Ingredients:*
8 slices bread
4 eggs
2 c. milk
1 t. vanilla
1/4 c. sugar
1/2 c. raisins
2 t. cinnamon
½ stick of butter
aluminum foil pan
aluminum foil

*Preparation:*
1. Melt the butter in an aluminum pan on the grill.
2. Beat together everything except the bread.
3. Tear the bread into little pieces and layer the bottom of the buttered pan with them.
4. Pour the egg mixture over the bread.
5. Cover the pan with aluminum foil and cook for 30-40 minutes.
6. Serve with maple syrup.

*Variation:*
- You can use leftover cake or muffins instead of bread. Cinnamon swirl bread is really good with this, too.

"The proof of the pudding is in the eating." – Miguel de Cervantes, *Don Quixote de la Mancha*

## Donuts

They're not really donuts, but you won't really care.

*Serves: 4-6*

*Ingredients:*
1 can refrigerated biscuit dough
butter
½ c. cinnamon sugar
paper bag

*Preparation:*
1. Melt 1 T. of butter in a skillet.
2. Drop a small piece of dough into the hot butter – about 1/3 of a biscuit – and cook it for 2-3 minutes on each side, until golden brown.
3. When it's done, shake it in a paper bag with the cinnamon sugar in it.
4. Serve these warm, so either eat them as you make them, or keep them warm by the fire.

"Cinnamon. It should be on tables at restaurants along with salt and pepper. Anytime anyone says, 'Oh, this is so good. What's in it?' The answer invariably comes back, 'Cinnamon'. 'Cinnamon'. Again and again." – Jerry Seinfeld

## Cinnamon Balls

This is like cinnamon donuts with the cinnamon on the inside!

*Serves: 4-6*

*Ingredients:*
2 c. Bisquick
¼ c. brown sugar
1 t. cinnamon
¼ c. raisins
water
butter

*Preparation:*
1. Grease a skillet with butter.
2. Add water little by little to the Bisquick, stirring carefully, until you have a dough – not too sticky.
3. Moisten your hands. Take a handful of dough and make a hole in the center. Spoon brown sugar and raisins into the hole and sprinkle them with cinnamon.
4. Pinch the hole closed and place the ball of dough in the skillet.
5. Repeat with the rest of the dough until the skillet is full (the dough balls will touch).
6. Cover the skillet and cook it over medium heat for 20-30 minutes.
7. Serve with butter.

*Variations:*
- Add nuts.
- You could make a savory version of this and fill the hole with cheese and meat and veggies.

*TIP:*
- Baking over an open fire is an art form. Check your skillet often and experiment with placement on the coals.

"Affluence separates people. Poverty knits 'em together. You got some sugar and I don't; I borrow some of yours. Next month you might not have any flour; well, I'll give you some of mine." – Ray Charles

## Monkey Bread

Invented in America, and we don't even have monkeys.

*Serves: 4-6*

*Ingredients:*
1 tube refrigerated biscuit dough
½ c. brown sugar
2 t. cinnamon
butter

*Preparation:*
1. Grease a skillet or Dutch Oven with butter.
2. Let the kids mix the sugar and cinnamon together in a plastic bag.
3. Have the kids pull biscuits off the roll and shake each biscuit in the bag of cinnamon sugar.
4. Place the biscuits in the skillet or Dutch Oven.
5. Dot each biscuit with butter.
6. Cover and cook the bread over medium heat for 20-30 minutes. If you cook this in a Dutch Oven, pile hot coals on top with your camp shovel.

"Cooking is like love. It should be entered into with abandon or not at all."
– Harriet Van Horne

## Ice Cream in a Can

You can buy a plastic ice cream maker ball (I think LL Bean carries them) or you can do it old school, like this. To procure a big, 3 lb. coffee can, try a diner or a college cafeteria. Or you can use a clean paint or spackle can the right size.

*Serves: 4*

*Ingredients:*
1 pint half and half or milk
1/2 c. sugar
1 t. vanilla extract
1 c. strawberries
crushed ice
rock salt
1 clean 1-lb. coffee can with the plastic lid
1 clean 3-lb. coffee can with the plastic lid
duct tape

*Preparation:*
1. Put the half and half or milk, sugar, vanilla and strawberries into a 1 lb. coffee can and mix it well.
2. Put the lid on the coffee can and tape it shut with duct tape.
3. Put the one lb. coffee can into the 3 lb. coffee can and surround it with crushed ice and rock salt.
4. Put the lid on the 3 lb. can and secure it with duct tape.
5. Have your kids roll the can back and forth for about 20 minutes.
6. Check the ice cream – if it isn't done, add more ice and rock salt and roll it for another 10-20 minutes.
7. Serve the ice cream in bowls.

*Variations:*
- Instead of fruit, add 2 T. of chocolate syrup to make chocolate ice cream, and serve the ice cream with extra chocolate syrup, if desired.
- Use any other kind of fruit or flavoring you can think of. Peanut butter springs to mind.

"Without ice cream, there would be darkness and chaos." – Don Kardong

## Ice Cream in a Ziploc Bag

Forget your coffee cans? Never fear, Ziploc is here!

*Serves: 1*

*Ingredients:*
½ c. half and half or milk
2 t. sugar
¼ t. vanilla extract
2 or 3 strawberries, chopped
crushed ice
8 T. rock salt
1 large sandwich size Ziploc bag
1 gallon size Ziploc bag

*Preparation:*
1. Put the half and half or milk, sugar, vanilla and strawberries into the sandwich size Ziploc bag.
2. Zip the air out of the baggie and mix well.
3. Put the sandwich baggie of ice cream mixture into the larger Ziploc bag and surround it with crushed ice and rock salt.
4. Close the larger bag and shake the whole package, being careful to not burst the bags.
5. Shake the bags for about 10 minutes and check the ice cream. If it isn't done, add more ice and rock salt and shake it for another 5-10 minutes.
6. Eat the ice cream right out of the little baggie, but wipe the outside off before opening it so you don't eat any of the rock salt by mistake.

"My advice to you is not to inquire why or whither, but just enjoy your ice cream while it's on your plate. That's my philosophy." – Thornton Wilder

## Dulce de Leche

My mother-in-law, Judy, introduced me to this simply perfect recipe for Dulce de Leche. Try not to explode the can, OK?

*Serves: 4-6 or one person hiding in the car with a spoon*

*Ingredients:*
1 can sweetened, condensed milk

*Preparation:*
1. Put an <u>unopened</u> can of sweetened, condensed milk in a pot of room temperature water (not boiling, or the can might explode) and bring to a vigorous simmer.
2. Simmer for three hours.

*Dulce de Leche*

# MEAL PLANS

# MEAL PLANS

**Weekend Meal Plan (3 nights/4 days)**

Having a plan means you don't over-buy or over-pack food – and it's fun to look forward to the special camping food everyone loves!

We put out fruit at most meals and snacks. A cut up apple always gets eaten!

|       | BREAKFAST | LUNCH | DINNER | SNACKS & DESSERTS |
|---|---|---|---|---|
| DAY 1 | *At home* | *Takeout en route* | •Steak<br>•Spider Dogs<br>•Green salad<br>•Italian bread | •Nachos<br>•S'Mores |
| DAY 2 | •Paper Bag Eggs<br>•Instant Grits | •Steak Tacos (with leftovers)<br>•Bread salad (with leftovers) | •Stew in a Can<br>•Baked Potatoes<br>•Bread on a stick | •Warm Granola Bars<br>•Chocolate Cake Oranges |
| DAY 3 | •Sausages<br>•Apple Pancakes | •Mac 'n' Cheese<br>•Pigs in Blankets<br>•Leftover Chocolate Cake | •Foil Packets for the kids<br>•Oxtail Stew for the grownups<br>•Pink Salad<br>•Biscuits | •Gorp<br>•Popcorn in foil packets<br>•Pineapple Upside Down Cake |
| DAY 4 | •Cowboy Eggs<br>•Leftover Pineapple Upside Down Cake | •Pie Iron Pizzas<br>•Corn on the Cob | *At home* | •Scooby Snacks |

# THE REAL FAMILY CAMPING COOKBOOK

## A Whole Week's Meal Plan (6 nights/7 days)

Dream vacation: a whole week of camping.

| | BREAKFAST | LUNCH | DINNER | SNACKS & DESSERTS |
|---|---|---|---|---|
| DAY 1 | *At home* | *Takeout en route* | •Steak<br>•Spider Dogs<br>•Green salad<br>Italian bread | •Nachos<br>•S'Mores |
| DAY 2 | •Hot Dog Bun French Toast | •Steak Tacos (with leftovers)<br>•Bread salad (with leftovers) | •Stew in a Can<br>•Baked Potatoes<br>•Bread on a stick | •Warm Granola Bars<br>•Chocolate Cake Oranges |
| DAY 3 | •Paper Bag Eggs<br>•Instant Grits | •Mac 'n' Cheese<br>•Pigs in Blankets<br>•Leftover Chocolate Cake | •Foil Packets for the kids<br>•Oxtail Stew for the grownups<br>•Pink Salad<br>•Biscuits | •Gorp<br>•Pineapple Upside Down Cake |
| DAY 4 | •Cowboy Eggs<br>•Leftover Pineapple Upside Down Cake | •Pie Iron Pizzas<br>•Corn on the Cob | •Clam Chowder<br>•Bannock | •String Cheese Logs<br>•Broom Handle Eclairs |
| DAY 5 | •Apple Pancakes | •Veggie Stew | •Dutch Oven Pizza | •Wormy Apples<br>•Craisy Cakes |
| DAY 6 | •Banana Tacos<br>•Campfire Applesauce | •Fried Rice-A-Roni | •Glop | •Popcorn in foil packets<br>•Monkey Bread |
| DAY 7 | •Monkey Bread French Toast | •Grilled Cheese and Curry | *At home* | •Scooby Snacks |

## ACKNOWLEDGMENTS

Heartfelt thanks to Curtis Allen of CAC Digital Arts, who produced the original ebook of the same title.

## ILLUSTRATIONS

All the illustrations in this book are based on real photos we took on camping trips. To be honest, our photos were not necessarily print quality, taken mostly on our phones and only for family memories. So to translate them into print and for a more consistent look, we turned them into line drawings. Hope you like them!

## ABOUT THE AUTHOR

*Photo: Jennifer Young*

Maggie da Silva is a writer and avid camper. Her enthusiasm for camping stems from her experience camping as a child, then camping with her own children. She has camped on steep mountainsides, scrubby campgrounds with dirty lakes, and, of course, in raging thunderstorms!

She believes that camping and nature must be accessible and open to all people.

She blogs about all things camping at www.realfamilycamping.blogspot.com, and you can find her on Twitter, Instagram and Facebook as @realfamilytime.

# NOTES

# NOTES

# NOTES

# NOTES

Made in the USA
Middletown, DE
07 December 2020